DATA SCIENCE AND BIG DATA

Data Science and Big Data Analytics:

Unlocking the Power of Information

LIAM MORGAN

Table of Contents

Introduction

The power of data has become a force that propels innovation, decision-making, and industry transformation in our quickly changing world. The digital age has created a new massive information generation, collection, and storage era. The amount of data available is enormous, but it will take advanced methods and resources to fully realize its potential. Welcome to "Data Science and Big Data: Data Science and Big Data Analytics - Unlocking the Power of Information."

Modern civilization now depends heavily on data, which shapes how companies run, how governments enact laws, and how individuals go about their everyday lives. Data-driven insights are becoming more and more crucial for businesses to obtain a competitive edge, from retail and healthcare to banking and entertainment. Today's information-driven world depends on the ability to draw meaningful conclusions and patterns from data, which drives innovation and advancement.

At the heart of this change is data science, the art of turning raw data into insights that can be used. To extract useful information from complicated datasets, this multidisciplinary area incorporates aspects of computer science, machine learning, statistics, and domain expertise. Data scientists are the alchemists of today, using creative problem-solving and analytical methods to transform data into gold.

At the same time, big data has become a significant idea. Data is being produced at a never-before-seen scale and speed due to the widespread use of digital devices, social media, and sensors. Volume, Velocity, and Variety are the 3Vs that define big data. Because processing, analyzing, and deriving insights from these enormous datasets requires specialized tools and procedures, it offers both an opportunity and a difficulty.

The convergence of Big Data Analytics and Data Science forms the core of this revolutionary environment. This e-book serves as a guide to help you comprehend and maximize the power of these two forces. This e-book can help you unleash the potential of information, whether you're a seasoned data expert looking to improve your skills or a novice eager to get started in this exciting sector. It will provide you with the knowledge and resources you need.

In the upcoming chapters, we shall detail the foundations of Big Data Analytics and Data Science. We'll look at the approaches, strategies, and tools that help us interpret data and find insightful information. This e-book will take you on a journey through data-driven discovery, covering everything from the fundamentals of data types and formats to the intricacies of deep learning and natural language processing.

This e-book includes content for everyone, regardless of their level of interest in the field of machine learning algorithms, the difficulties of managing massive amounts of data, or the ethical implications of data use. By the time you finish, you'll have a firm understanding of the principles and tools that underpin Big Data analytics and data science.

As you begin your journey through the pages of "Data Science and Big Data: Data Science and Big Data Analytics - Unlocking the Power of Information," never forget that you hold the power of data. The knowledge acquired from these pages will enable you to drive innovation, make well-informed decisions, and add to the expanding body of data-driven expertise.

Let's start exploring the exciting fields of data science and big data analytics and jointly harness the power of information.

Chapter I

Foundations of Data Science

Understanding Data Types and Formats

In the digital age, data is the cornerstone of modern society, driving decision-making, innovation, and progress across many industries. As the data volume grows exponentially, it becomes imperative to comprehend the intricacies of data types and formats. These fundamental aspects lay the foundation for effective data manipulation, analysis, and interpretation, forming the bedrock of data science and its applications.

At its core, data is a representation of information. Data types define the nature and characteristics of the information being stored, processed, and analyzed. They encompass a wide range of categories, each serving a specific purpose in data science. The common data types include integers, floating-point numbers, strings, booleans, etc. Integers, for instance, represent whole numbers, while floating-point numbers accommodate decimals. Strings encompass textual information, and booleans signify binary states of true or false. Data types are essential as they dictate how data can be operated upon, ensuring consistency and accuracy throughout the analytical process.

One crucial distinction among data types lies in the division between categorical and numerical data. Categorical data consists of discrete, non-numeric values that represent categories or labels. These values lack any inherent numerical meaning and include variables like gender, color, and product names. On the other hand, numerical data encompasses values with quantitative significance. It is further divided into two subcategories: discrete and continuous. Discrete numerical data comprises distinct, separate values (e.g., the number of products sold), while continuous numerical data spans a range of values with potential decimal points (e.g., temperature readings). Understanding this distinction is vital as it influences the choice of analytical techniques and visualizations employed for data exploration.

Temporal information is a critical facet of data that often holds intrinsic value. Dates and times are omnipresent in datasets, whether recording transaction timestamps, event occurrences, or sensor readings. These values are stored in specific date and time formats, ensuring accurate representation and manipulation. Common formats include ISO 8601, which presents dates and times in a standardized manner, and Unix timestamps, which represent the number of seconds since January 1, 1970. The proper handling of date and time formats is pivotal to uncovering temporal patterns, trends, and insights buried within the data.

Data comes in diverse formats, and understanding the distinction between structured and unstructured data is essential. Structured data is highly organized, residing within rows and columns, akin to a spreadsheet or a relational database. Unstructured data, however, lacks a predetermined structure, making it more challenging to analyze. Examples of unstructured data contain text documents, images, audio recordings, and videos. As unstructured data becomes increasingly prevalent, techniques like computer vision and natural language processing are employed to extract valuable insights from this untamed information.

Data formats are crucial to determine how data is stored, transmitted, and accessed. Choosing the appropriate format impacts compatibility, storage efficiency, and processing speed. Common data formats include CSV (Comma-Separated Values), XML (eXtensible Markup Language), Parquet, and JSON (JavaScript Object Notation). Each format has strengths and weaknesses, making the selection a pivotal decision affecting data interchange and analysis. For instance, CSV is human-readable and widely supported, while Parquet is optimized for big data processing, minimizing storage space and boosting query performance.

In conclusion, data types and formats lay the groundwork for effective data manipulation and analysis. Understanding these fundamental concepts is paramount for anyone venturing into data science. Categorical and numerical data, date and time formats, structured and unstructured data, and the significance of data formats collectively contribute to the mosaic of knowledge required to unlock the power of information. In a world inundated with data, these concepts serve as guiding principles, enabling us to navigate the complex landscape of data-driven insights with precision and insight.

Introduction to Data Collection and Cleaning

In the age of information, data has emerged as a pivotal driver of decision-making, innovation, and progress across diverse fields. However, the raw data is rarely pristine; it often requires careful collection and rigorous cleaning to extract valuable insights accurately. Data collection and cleaning is a foundational step in the journey of data science, enabling analysts and researchers to work with high-quality, reliable data that forms the basis of informed decision-making and meaningful analysis.

Data collection marks the starting point of the data science lifecycle. It systematically gathers information from various sources, from structured databases to unstructured text, images, and sensor readings. Data collection aims to obtain a comprehensive and representative sample that reflects the real-world phenomena being studied. Proper data collection methodologies ensure that the insights drawn from the data accurately reflect the underlying trends, patterns, and behaviors. Additionally, ethical considerations such as informed consent and data privacy must be considered during the collection process.

Data collection methodologies are diverse, each tailored to the nature of the research question and the data collection type. Surveys involve gathering individual responses through questionnaires, interviews, or online forms. They are ideal for capturing subjective information, opinions, and preferences. Experiments, on the other hand, involve controlled manipulation of variables to understand cause-and-effect relationships. This method is common in scientific research, enabling researchers to make causal inferences. Other methods include observational studies, where data is collected by observing subjects in their natural environment, and data mining, where patterns are extracted from existing datasets.

While data collection is essential, it comes with its share of challenges. One major concern is the potential for bias. Bias can emerge from various sources, such as sampling methods that favor certain groups, leading to results that do not accurately represent the broader population. Quality assurance is another critical consideration, as errors or inconsistencies in data collection can propagate throughout the analysis process, leading to misleading conclusions. Mitigating bias and ensuring data quality requires careful planning, standardized protocols, and thorough validation procedures.

Once data is collected, it often requires cleaning to transform it into a usable form. Raw data can be riddled with errors, missing values, and inconsistencies that hinder meaningful analysis. Data cleaning involves a series of processes to identify and rectify these issues. Missing data, for instance, can be attributed using statistical techniques, while outliers—data points that deviate significantly from the norm—can be assessed for accuracy and relevance. Cleaning also involves standardizing formats, correcting typos, and ensuring consistency in categorical variables.

Data cleaning techniques vary, ranging from manual inspection to automated algorithms. Manual inspection involves visually inspecting the data for errors, which can be time-consuming and subjective. Automated methods, such as outlier detection algorithms and imputation techniques, expedite the process and reduce human bias. Data validation rules can also be applied to identify implausible values or inconsistencies. The selection of technique depends on the complexity of the data and the resources available.

Data cleaning is not a one-time endeavor but an iterative process intertwined with data analysis. As analysts explore the data and uncover patterns, they may identify additional cleaning steps that need to be taken. Furthermore, cleaning is closely connected to domain knowledge; understanding the context in which the data was collected is crucial for making informed decisions about handling inconsistencies or anomalies. Iterative data cleaning ensures that the insights drawn from the data are accurate, reliable, and unbiased.

The significance of data collection and cleaning cannot be overstated in the ever-expanding landscape of data science. These initial steps lay the groundwork for meaningful analysis, informed decision-making, and innovative breakthroughs. Successful data collection methodologies capture the essence of the phenomena being studied, while rigorous data cleaning unveils the hidden patterns buried within the noise. As the world generates an unprecedented volume of data, mastering the art of data collection and cleaning is essential for those seeking to navigate the complexities of the data-driven era. By embracing these foundational practices, we can ensure that the insights derived from data are accurate, actionable, and instrumental in shaping a better, more informed world.

Exploring Descriptive Statistics

The journey from raw data to meaningful insights often begins with closely examining descriptive statistics in data science. These statistical measures provide a snapshot of a dataset's key characteristics and patterns, offering valuable insights that pave the way for deeper analysis and informed decision-making. By distilling complex data into easily understandable summaries, descriptive statistics empower analysts to uncover trends, distributions, and relationships beneath the surface.

Descriptive statistics serve as a window into the heart of the data. They condense voluminous datasets into concise summaries revealing the central tendencies and variations. These summaries are essential for communicating the essence of the data to both technical and non-technical audiences. Whether exploring a dataset for the first time or preparing it for further analysis, descriptive statistics lay the groundwork for extracting meaningful insights.

Measures of central tendency offer insights into where the data cluster around a central value. By adding up all of the values and dividing by the total number of observations, one may determine the mean, or average. It provides a general sense of the dataset's central location. The median, which is the middle value when the data is sorted, is less influenced by outliers, making it suitable for skewed distributions. The value that occurs the most frequently is represented by the mode. These measures collectively provide a sense of the data's central concentration.

While measures of central tendency offer insight into the center of the data, dispersion measures shed light on the spread or variability of the data points. The range, a simple measure, represents the difference between the maximum and minimum values. The variance and standard deviation quantify the average squared difference between each data point and the mean, providing a more comprehensive understanding of dispersion. It is possible to compare datasets with various scales by using the coefficient of variation, which may be computed by dividing the standard deviation by the mean.

Descriptive statistics also delve into the shape of data distributions. Skewness measures the asymmetry of a distribution. A positive skew indicates a long tail on the right, while a negative skew has a long tail on the left. Kurtosis assesses the "tailedness" of a distribution. High kurtosis suggests heavy tails and more extreme values, while low kurtosis indicates a flatter distribution. These measures provide insights into the departure of the data distribution from a normal (bell-shaped) curve.

Visual representations are crucial in enhancing the understanding of descriptive statistics. Histograms provide a graphical depiction of data distribution, showing the frequency of values within different intervals, or bins. Box plots, also known as box-and-whisker plots, offer a visual summary of the data's central tendency, dispersion, and outliers. These visuals complement descriptive statistics by visually representing the data's characteristics.

Descriptive statistics extend beyond individual variables, encompassing the exploration of relationships between variables. The degree to which two variables change together is measured by covariance. Positive covariance indicates that as one variable increases, the other also tends to increase, while negative covariance signifies an inverse relationship. Correlation, a normalized measure, ranges between -1 and 1, depicting the strength and direction of linear relationships between variables.

Descriptive statistics provide a holistic view of data, allowing analysts to grasp the nuances of a dataset without delving into complex modeling techniques. These statistical measures enable decision-makers to identify trends, anomalies, and relationships influencing outcomes. Whether evaluating customer purchasing patterns, analyzing financial data, or exploring healthcare trends, descriptive statistics are the gateway to uncovering insights that drive strategic decisions.

In the intricate landscape of data science, descriptive statistics are the foundation upon which deeper analysis is built. These statistical measures transform raw data into actionable insights, painting a comprehensive picture of the data's landscape. As we delve into measures of central tendency, dispersion, distribution shapes, and relationships, we unlock the potential to extract knowledge that guides decision-making and fuels innovation. Descriptive statistics are analytical tools and the storytellers of data, revealing narratives that influence the course of our data-driven world. By mastering the art of descriptive statistics, we equip ourselves with the tools to uncover hidden truths and make informed choices that shape our future.

Basics of Data Visualization

In the modern era of data-driven decision-making, communicating insights effectively is as crucial as the analytical skills themselves. This is where data visualization steps onto the stage. Data visualization is the art of transforming raw data into visual representations that convey complex information intuitively and compellingly. By creating visual narratives that transcend the boundaries of numbers and statistics, data visualization empowers analysts, researchers, and decision-makers to glean insights, detect patterns, and communicate findings with clarity and impact.

Humans are inherently visual beings, and our brains are wired to quickly process and understand visual information. Data visualization harnesses this natural inclination, translating abstract data points into visual elements that are more accessible and memorable. By representing data through graphs, charts, maps, and diagrams, we transform data from mere numbers and words into a language that speaks directly to our cognition, enabling us to grasp complex concepts and relationships at a glance.

Many data visualization techniques exist, each suited to different types of data and the insights we seek to extract. For instance, bar charts and line graphs illustrate trends and variables' comparisons. Pie charts convey proportions and percentages in a visually digestible format. Scatter plots reveal relationships and correlations between variables. Heatmaps depict patterns and variations in large datasets using color gradients. Geographic maps show spatial distributions and regional trends. Choosing the correct type of visualization depends on the data's nature and the story we aim to tell.

Visualizing data distributions is essential for understanding the underlying patterns and characteristics. Histograms divide data into bins and display the frequency of data points within each bin, highlighting the shape of the distribution. Box plots, on the other hand, summarize key statistical measures such as median, quartiles, and outliers. These visualizations illuminate the central tendencies and spread of data, aiding in detecting anomalies and assessing data quality.

As technology evolves, so do the capabilities of data visualization. Interactive visualizations take engagement to the next level by allowing users to explore data dynamically. With interactive elements such as tooltips, filters, and zoom features, users can drill down into specific data points, view additional information, and uncover insights tailored to their interests. Interactive dashboards provide a holistic view of multiple visualizations, enabling users to understand complex datasets in real time comprehensively.

Effective data visualization is not only about creating aesthetically pleasing visuals; it's about conveying information accurately and meaningfully. Design principles play a critical role in achieving this goal. Clarity, simplicity, and consistency are paramount. Labels, titles, and legends should be clear and concise, guiding the viewer's interpretation. Color choices must be deliberate, ensuring that they aid understanding rather than confuse. The balance between aesthetics and functionality is essential, as overly complex visuals can obscure insights.

While data visualization is a powerful tool for communication, it comes with ethical responsibilities. Visualizations should be honest and accurate representations of the data. Manipulating visual elements, such as altering scales or selectively displaying data points, can lead to misleading interpretations. Context is equally crucial; visualizations should provide a comprehensive view without cherry-picking data to support a specific narrative. Transparency in data sources, methodologies, and limitations fosters trust in the insights presented.

Beyond the technical aspects, data visualization is a form of storytelling. Visualizations should be organized into coherent narratives that guide the viewer through the data's insights. A well-structured visualization tells a story that begins with an introduction, unfolds with insights and discoveries, and culminates in a conclusion or actionable takeaway. Annotations and annotations provide context and guide the viewer's attention, ensuring that the narrative is clear and compelling.

Data visualization is a bridge that connects the analytical realm to human cognition. By harnessing the power of visuals, we unlock the potential to convey complex information, uncover hidden patterns, and make informed decisions. From simple bar charts to intricate interactive dashboards, data visualization offers various tools for effectively communicating insights. By embracing design principles, ethical considerations, and the art of storytelling, we wield the power to illuminate the data landscape, enabling us to navigate the complexities of the data-driven world with clarity and confidence. As technology advances and data proliferates, data visualization becomes increasingly indispensable, enabling us to transform data into knowledge and reshape how we understand and interact with our data-rich reality.

Chapter II

Introduction to Big Data

Characteristics and Challenges of Big Data

In the digital age, the explosion of data production and consumption has given rise to Big Data—a phenomenon that has transformed the landscape of information management and analysis. Big Data represents a massive volume of data and a paradigm shift in how we perceive, collect, process, and derive value from this information. As we delve into the characteristics and challenges of Big Data, we uncover a world of unprecedented opportunities and complexities that require innovative approaches and solutions.

The most conspicuous characteristic of Big Data is its sheer volume. Traditional databases and tools struggle to handle the scale of data generated daily by myriad sources, including social media, sensors, and transactions. The petabytes and exabytes that characterize Big Data necessitate scalable storage solutions and distributed computing frameworks. This volume-driven challenge requires the development of specialized systems capable of accommodating and processing data at a magnitude unimaginable just a few years ago.

Data is no longer static; it flows at an unprecedented velocity. Real-time information from sources like social media updates, stock market fluctuations, and sensor data requires rapid analysis to derive meaningful insights. The challenge lies in processing and also analyzing this data in near-real time to enable timely decision-making. Technologies like stream processing and complex event processing are essential to keep up with the fast-paced nature of data velocity.

Big Data is not limited to structured databases; it encompasses various data types, including structured, semi-structured, and unstructured data. This variety includes text, images, videos, audio, and more. Traditional relational databases fall short in handling this diverse range of data formats. Tools and techniques that can process, analyze, and extract value from unstructured and semi-structured data are essential for deriving insights from the full spectrum of available information.

The veracity of Big Data refers to the data's accuracy, reliability, and trustworthiness. As data volume, velocity, and variety increase, maintaining data quality becomes a challenge. Inaccuracies, inconsistencies, and biases can infiltrate the data, leading to faulty conclusions. Data cleaning and preprocessing are critical steps to address veracity challenges, ensuring that the insights drawn from the data are accurate and reliable.

The variability of Big Data highlights the dynamic nature of data sources and formats. Data can exhibit volume, velocity, and quality fluctuations over time, making it difficult to standardize and process consistently. Dealing with this variability requires adaptability and agility in data processing frameworks. The ability to handle changes in data patterns and sources is crucial for deriving meaningful insights in a constantly evolving data landscape.

Ultimately, the value of Big Data lies in its potential to yield insights that drive informed decisions and innovation. The challenge is to extract actionable knowledge from the immense sea of data. Advanced analytics techniques, including machine learning, data mining, and predictive modeling, are instrumental in uncovering hidden patterns, correlations, and trends within Big Data. Transforming raw data into valuable insights is the pinnacle of Big Data's potential.

While Big Data offers unprecedented opportunities, it also presents formidable challenges that require innovative solutions. The first challenge is data storage and management. Traditional databases struggle to handle the volume and variety of Big Data. Distributed storage systems like Hadoop Distributed File System (HDFS) and cloud-based solutions provide scalable storage capabilities. However, managing and querying these vast datasets efficiently remains a challenge.

Another challenge is data processing. Traditional batch processing methods are ill-suited for real-time data streams. Big Data processing frameworks like Apache Spark offer in-memory, parallel processing capabilities that accelerate data analysis.

However, programming complex algorithms and optimizing performance require specialized skills.

Data privacy and security are major concerns in the era of Big Data. The massive amount of collected personal and sensitive data raises ethical and legal questions about data ownership, consent, and protection. Adhering to data privacy regulations and implementing robust security measures is essential to build trust and ensure compliance.

Integration and interoperability are challenges as data comes from diverse sources and in various formats. Siloed data prevents organizations from harnessing the full potential of Big Data. Developing data integration solutions that enable seamless data flow and cross-platform compatibility is crucial for holistic analysis.

The skills gap poses yet another challenge. The field of Big Data demands expertise in data science, machine learning, distributed computing, and more. There is a shortage of professionals with the necessary skills to navigate the complexities of Big Data, making talent acquisition and skill development a critical concern.

Big Data is a multifaceted phenomenon with characteristics that demand innovative processing, analysis, and value extraction approaches. The challenges it presents are as diverse as the data itself. Organizations and individuals that embrace the potential of Big Data while addressing its challenges stand to gain a competitive edge through data-driven decision-making, innovation, and improved insights. By harnessing the power of advanced technologies, interdisciplinary collaboration, and ethical practices, we can navigate the complex terrain of Big Data and unlock its transformative potential for a data-rich future.

Big Data 3Vs: Volume, Velocity, and Variety

Data has become the lifeblood of innovation in the modern digital landscape, driving decision-making, insights, and advancements across various industries. The term "Big Data" encapsulates the massive scale of information generated and the complexity of managing and deriving value from this abundance of data. At the heart of understanding Big Data are the three fundamental dimensions known as the 3Vs: Volume, Velocity, and Variety. These dimensions serve as guiding pillars that define the unique challenges as well as opportunities posed by the era of data abundance.

The first V, Volume, refers to the sheer magnitude of data being produced at an unprecedented rate. Traditional databases and tools that were once sufficient for managing data are now overwhelmed by the deluge of information generated by sources such as social media, Internet of Things (IoT) devices, and online transactions. The volume of data is measured in petabytes, exabytes, and beyond—previously unfathomable scales. This monumental increase in data volume necessitates advanced storage solutions, distributed computing frameworks, and cloud infrastructure to manage, store, and process data effectively.

Velocity is the speed at which data is generated, processed, and analyzed. The days of batch processing and delayed analysis are giving way to the demand for real-time insights. Data streams from social media updates, stock market data, and sensor readings require rapid processing to detect trends, anomalies, and patterns as they unfold. The challenge lies in harnessing data velocity to make timely decisions and derive actionable insights. Technologies like stream processing and complex event processing are essential to keep up with the speed of data generation and ensure that insights are derived promptly.

Variety encompasses the diverse types and formats of data contributing to Big Data's complexity. In addition to traditional structured data in relational databases, Big Data includes semi-structured and unstructured data, such as text, images, videos, audio, and more. The rise of multimedia content, social media interactions, and sensor data introduces many formats that defy conventional storage and processing methods. Successfully harnessing the potential of Big Data requires tools, algorithms, and techniques that can accommodate and derive insights from this heterogeneous landscape.

The interplay of the 3Vs—Volume, Velocity, and Variety—creates a synergy that characterizes the challenges and opportunities of Big Data. The volume and velocity of data contribute to the variety, as diverse sources generate a massive influx of information at unparalleled speeds. This interdependence elevates the complexity of Big Data analytics, requiring innovative solutions to manage, process, and analyze the diversity of data points in real-time.

Addressing the 3Vs necessitates a holistic approach that combines technological advancements, data management strategies, and analytical methodologies.

Each V presents distinct challenges and opportunities in the realm of Big Data. The volume of data necessitates scalable storage solutions and robust data management techniques. Cloud computing and distributed storage systems like Hadoop HDFS enable organizations to handle massive datasets efficiently. The velocity of data requires real-time processing capabilities and advanced analytics tools. Technologies such as Apache Spark and streaming frameworks offer the ability to process data in motion, enabling rapid insights. The variety of data demands flexible data integration and analysis methods. Techniques like the natural language processing and image recognition empower organizations to extract unstructured and semi-structured data insights.

The synergy of the 3Vs opens doors to novel applications and innovations. Organizations can harness Big Data to understand customer behavior better, predict market trends, optimize supply chains, and improve healthcare outcomes. Real-time insights enable timely interventions and informed decision-making. Diverse data sources empower researchers to uncover patterns and correlations previously hidden. The 3Vs converge to drive advancements in artificial intelligence, machine learning, and predictive analytics, fostering a data-driven culture of innovation.

The 3Vs—Volume, Velocity, and Variety—constitute the cornerstone of the Big Data paradigm. They define the challenges and opportunities that shape the landscape of modern data analytics. As data continues to expand and diversify, organizations and individuals must adapt their strategies, technologies, and methodologies to harness the power of Big Data effectively. By embracing scalable storage solutions, real-time processing capabilities, and flexible analysis techniques, we unlock the potential to extract insights, uncover patterns, and drive innovation in a world fueled by data. As technology evolves and data increases, the 3Vs remain a guiding framework that empowers us to navigate the complexities of the data-driven era and unlock the full potential of information abundance.

Technologies and Tools for Handling Big Data

In an age marked by the relentless growth of data, the challenges of processing, storing, and deriving insights from massive datasets have spurred the development of various technologies and tools. As the volume, velocity, and variety of data expand, these technologies have become essential for businesses, researchers, and organizations seeking to harness the power of Big Data. From distributed storage systems to advanced analytics platforms, these tools enable efficient data management, real-time processing, and actionable insights. In this section, we will explore some of the key technologies and tools that play a pivotal role in handling the complexities of Big Data.

The sheer volume of data generated in the digital age has outpaced the capabilities of traditional storage solutions. Distributed storage systems have emerged as a solution to this challenge, enabling the seamless expansion of storage capacity by distributing data across multiple servers or nodes. The Hadoop Distributed File System (HDFS) stands out among these systems. HDFS breaks data into blocks and distributes them across a cluster of machines, providing fault tolerance and scalability. This technology enables organizations to store and manage massive datasets efficiently, providing the foundation for processing and analysis.

Once data is stored, the challenge lies in processing and analyzing it efficiently. MapReduce, a programming model pioneered by Google and popularized by Apache Hadoop, addresses this challenge by enabling parallel data processing across distributed clusters. It divides tasks into map and reduce phases, allowing for the simultaneous execution of tasks on multiple nodes. MapReduce has revolutionized the field of data processing, making it feasible to analyze large datasets that would be impractical using traditional methods.

While MapReduce revolutionized batch processing, the need for real-time insights spurred the development of Apache Spark. Spark is an open-source, cluster-computing framework that offers in-memory data processing capabilities. Unlike the disk-based approach of MapReduce, Spark stores data in memory, significantly accelerating data processing. It supports batch processing, interactive queries, machine learning, and streaming, making it a versatile tool for handling diverse data processing and analysis tasks.

Traditional relational databases are only sometimes well-suited for the unstructured and semi-structured data that characterize Big Data. NoSQL databases provide an alternative, offering flexibility and scalability for handling diverse data types. Types of NoSQL databases include document databases like MongoDB, column-family stores like Apache Cassandra, and graph databases like Neo4j. These databases cater to specific data needs, allowing organizations to choose the most suitable technology based on the nature of their data.

Data warehousing solutions offer a centralized repository for storing and managing structured data. While traditional data warehouses were limited in their capacity to handle Big Data, modern data warehousing technologies like Amazon Redshift and Google BigQuery leverage cloud infrastructure to scale up and manage large datasets efficiently. These solutions enable organizations to perform complex analytics and derive insights from vast structured data.

Machine learning and also artificial intelligence have emerged as potent tools for deriving insights from Big Data. Platforms like TensorFlow, PyTorch, and scikit-learn provide frameworks and libraries for developing machine learning models that can identify patterns, make predictions, and classify data. These platforms enable organizations to unlock valuable insights from data and automate decision-making processes.

The velocity of data streams demands real-time processing capabilities. Stream processing platforms like Apache Kafka and Apache Flink address this need by allowing organizations to process and analyze data as it is generated. These platforms enable real-time analytics, making it possible to detect trends, anomalies, and patterns as they occur.

The insights derived from Big Data are most impactful when effectively communicated to stakeholders. Visualization tools like Tableau, Power BI, and D3.js enable the creation of compelling visual representations of data. These tools transform complex data into intuitive visualizations, making it easier for technical and non-technical audiences to understand and interpret insights.

While these technologies and tools offer immense potential, their implementation is not without challenges. Integrating diverse tools into a coherent data ecosystem requires careful planning and coordination. Scalability, data security, and privacy considerations are paramount. The skills gap, wherein the demand for data professionals exceeds supply, poses a challenge for organizations seeking to leverage these tools effectively.

In the realm of Big Data, the technologies and tools discussed above drive innovation, insights, and progress. As the volume, velocity, and variety of data expand, these tools empower organizations to manage, process, and analyze data efficiently. Each technology serves a particular purpose in the journey from raw data to actionable insights, from distributed storage and real-time processing to machine learning and visualization. As we navigate the complex landscape of Big Data, these technologies will continue to evolve, enabling us to unlock the full potential of information abundance and shape a data-driven future.

Chapter III

Data Storage and Management

Relational Databases and SQL

In data management, relational databases and Structured Query Language (SQL) stand as the foundational pillars that have shaped how we store, retrieve, and manipulate structured data. Relational databases have revolutionized information storage, providing a structured framework for organizing data into tables, while SQL serves as the universal language that enables users to interact with these databases. This section explores the significance of relational databases and SQL in the data landscape, delving into their history, key concepts, advantages, and continued relevance in the era of Big Data.

The evolution of databases can be traced back to the early days of computing when flat-file systems dominated. However, the need for a more structured and efficient way to manage data led to the development of relational databases in the 1970s. E.F. Codd's relational model laid the foundation, introducing the concept of organizing data into tables with rows (records) and columns (attributes). This model marked a paradigm shift, providing a logical and mathematical framework for data management that transcended the limitations of flat-file systems.

Relational databases are built on a set of key concepts that define their structure and integrity. Tables, also known as relations, are the central building blocks. Each table consists of rows, where each row represents a record, and columns, which represent attributes or fields. Primary keys uniquely identify each record within a table, ensuring data integrity and enabling relationships between tables. Foreign keys establish relationships between tables, allowing for complex data retrieval. Normalization, a process that eliminates redundancy and ensures data integrity, is crucial in designing relational databases.

Relational databases offer numerous advantages that have cemented their role as the go-to solution for structured data management. One of the primary benefits is data integrity. The structure of relational databases enforces rules that prevent duplicate or inconsistent data, ensuring the accuracy and reliability of stored information. Additionally, relational databases provide flexibility through their ability to define relationships between tables, enabling efficient data retrieval through SQL queries. This relational model allows for complex data analysis while maintaining a consistent and organized data structure.

Structured Query Language (also known as SQL) is the language that bridges the gap between users and relational databases. It offers a standardized way to interact with databases, despite of the underlying database management system (DBMS). SQL allows users to perform various operations, including creating tables, inserting, updating, and deleting records, querying data, and defining database structures. Its declarative nature enables users to specify what they want to achieve, leaving the details of how the operation is executed to the DBMS.

SQL's versatility shines in its ability to manipulate data and retrieve database insights. The SELECT statement forms the backbone of querying, allowing users to retrieve specific data based on specified conditions. Joins enable users to combine data from multiple tables based on common keys, facilitating complex data analysis. Aggregation functions like COUNT, SUM, AVG, and GROUP BY enable users to perform calculations and summarize data. SQL's rich set of commands empowers users to retrieve, filter, sort, and transform data according to their needs.

In the face of the Big Data revolution, the relevance of relational databases and SQL remains resolute. While NoSQL databases and non-relational data models cater to unstructured and semi-structured data, relational databases thrive in structured data management scenarios. The structured nature of relational databases lends itself to applications like transaction processing, financial systems, and enterprise resource planning (ERP) systems, where data integrity and consistency are paramount.

While relational databases excel in structured data management, they face challenges in handling the volume, velocity, and variety of data characteristic of Big Data. Scalability is a concern, as traditional relational databases may struggle to handle the massive datasets generated by modern applications and IoT devices. However, advancements in database technologies, such as sharding, replication, and distributed databases, have mitigated some of these challenges, making it possible to scale relational databases to handle larger workloads.

Relational databases and SQL stand as cornerstones of data management, offering a structured, organized, and reliable approach to handling structured data. Their history, key concepts, and advantages have shaped the way organizations store, retrieve, and analyze information. In an era where data is generated and consumed at an unprecedented pace, the continued relevance of relational databases is evident. Their adaptability to evolving technologies and ability to provide data integrity and structured querying ensure they will remain a fundamental tool in the data landscape. As organizations navigate the complexities of data, relational databases and SQL continue to offer endless possibilities for structured data management and analysis.

NoSQL Databases: Types and Use Cases

In modern data management, the rise of unstructured and semi-structured data, coupled with the need for scalability and flexibility, has given birth to a diverse family of database systems known as NoSQL databases. NoSQL, which stands for "not only SQL," challenges the traditional relational database model by offering solutions catering to modern applications' unique requirements and Big Data scenarios. This section explores the types of NoSQL databases and delves into their respective use cases, showcasing the versatility and innovation these databases bring to the world of data management.

NoSQL databases encompass a range of database systems, each designed to address specific data management challenges. Four main categories of NoSQL databases stand out: document databases, key-value stores, column-family stores, and graph databases.

Document databases are designed to store, retrieve, and manage document-oriented data, such as JSON or XML. Each document can have a different structure, enabling developers to work with data that evolves over time. MongoDB, a popular document database, allows users to store complex data structures in a schema-less format. Document databases are well-suited for content management systems, e-commerce platforms, and applications dealing with user-generated content.

Key-value stores keep data in a simple key-value pair format. These databases are efficient regarding read and write operations and are often used for caching, session management, and real-time analytics. Redis is a widely used key-value store that excels in performance and supports various data structures, making it suitable for use cases like real-time data processing, leaderboards, and message queuing.

Column-family stores organize data into columns rather than rows, allowing for efficient data retrieval and storage. These databases excel in scenarios that require storing and retrieving large volumes of data across distributed clusters. Apache Cassandra, a prominent column-family store, is often used for time-series data, sensor data, and applications requiring high availability and scalability.

Graph databases focus on representing and querying data as graphs, with nodes representing entities and edges representing relationships between them. These databases excel in scenarios where understanding complex relationships is essential, such as social networks, recommendation systems, and fraud detection. Neo4j is a popular graph database known for its ability to traverse relationships efficiently and uncover insights from connected data.

NoSQL databases offer a world of possibilities in diverse application scenarios. They are particularly valuable when data structures are dynamic, massive data volumes, and high performance demands.

In content management systems, document databases shine by accommodating evolving content structures and facilitating fast retrieval of diverse data types. E-commerce platforms leverage key-value stores for caching product data, improving user experience by reducing response times. Column-family stores are essential in scenarios demanding scalability, such as sensor data storage and management in IoT applications. Graph databases excel in applications like social networks, where understanding relationships is crucial for generating recommendations and analyzing user behavior.

NoSQL databases also find utility in real-time analytics, where the need for rapid data processing is paramount. They power applications that require high availability and low latency, such as online gaming and financial systems. NoSQL databases contribute to the evolution of healthcare by enabling the management and analysis of electronic health records, medical imaging data, and patient information.

While NoSQL databases offer advantages in specific use cases, they are not without challenges. The lack of a standardized query language can make it challenging for developers to switch between different types of NoSQL databases. Data consistency and integrity can be complex to maintain in distributed and highly available environments. Scaling and migrating traditional databases to NoSQL solutions can also be intricate and require careful planning.

NoSQL databases have redefined the boundaries of data management, providing specialized solutions that cater to the diverse demands of modern applications. Their adaptability, scalability, and ability to handle unstructured and semi-structured data have opened new possibilities for innovation in data-intensive industries. By embracing document databases, key-value stores, column-family stores, and graph databases, organizations can harness the power of NoSQL to unlock insights, drive efficiency, and deliver exceptional user experiences. The NoSQL ecosystem is a testament to the dynamism of the data landscape, showcasing the breadth of solutions available to address the ever-evolving challenges of the digital era.

Introduction to Distributed File Systems (e.g., Hadoop HDFS)

In the era of Big Data, the challenge of storing, managing, and processing massive volumes of data has given rise to the concept of distributed file systems. These systems revolutionize how data is stored and accessed, providing a scalable and fault-tolerant solution to handle the immense data generated by modern applications and technologies. One prominent example of a distributed file system is Hadoop HDFS (Hadoop Distributed File System). This section explores the fundamentals of distributed file systems, delves into the architecture and features of Hadoop HDFS, and highlights their significance in addressing the challenges of the data-driven landscape.

Traditional file systems were designed to manage data on a single machine, which limited their scalability and storage capacity. The advent of distributed file systems addressed these limitations by spreading data across multiple machines or nodes, enabling efficient storage and retrieval of massive datasets. Distributed file systems tackle challenges related to data replication, fault tolerance, and parallel data processing, making them a foundational component of modern data infrastructure.

Hadoop HDFS, developed as part of the Apache Hadoop ecosystem, is a leading distributed file system renowned for its ability to handle the storage needs of Big Data applications. HDFS operates on a master-slave architecture, comprising two main components: the NameNode and the DataNodes.

The NameNode serves as the metadata repository, storing information about the file system's structure, permissions, and location of data blocks. It manages the namespace and coordinates access to files. On the other hand, DataNodes store the actual data blocks and replicate them for fault tolerance. The DataNodes communicate with the NameNode, reporting their health status and the data blocks they store.

Hadoop HDFS offers several key features, making it a robust solution for managing Big Data. One of its primary strengths is scalability. HDFS can be easily expanded as data volumes grow by adding more DataNodes to the cluster. This scalability allows organizations to accommodate increasing data demands without disrupting existing operations.

Fault tolerance is another critical feature of Hadoop HDFS. Data redundancy is achieved by replicating data blocks across multiple DataNodes. If a DataNode fails or becomes unavailable, the replicated blocks can still be accessed, ensuring data availability and minimizing downtime. The NameNode's metadata is also crucial for fault tolerance. Hadoop HDFS employs data replication and metadata backups to maintain data integrity and availability in the face of failures.

Hadoop HDFS's data distribution mechanism contributes to its efficiency and fault tolerance. Large files are divided into smaller fixed-size blocks, typically 128 MB or 256 MB in size. These blocks are distributed across DataNodes in the cluster. Each block is replicated across multiple DataNodes to ensure redundancy. This approach optimizes data transfer and storage and minimizes the impact of hardware failures.

Hadoop HDFS's architecture and features make it an ideal solution for a broad range of use cases in the Big Data landscape. Analytical processing, where large datasets are processed to extract insights, benefits from HDFS's distributed and parallel processing capabilities. Batch processing, data warehousing, and ETL (Extract, Transform, Load) operations are also well-suited for Hadoop HDFS. The system's fault tolerance ensures that data remains available even in the event of hardware failures, contributing to the reliability of data-intensive applications.

Moreover, Hadoop HDFS is an integral part of the larger Hadoop ecosystem, which includes frameworks like Apache Spark for in-memory data processing and Apache Hive for data warehousing and querying. These technologies complement HDFS's capabilities, creating a comprehensive ecosystem for handling data storage, processing, and analysis.

While Hadoop HDFS has been instrumental in addressing Big Data challenges, it has limitations. Its architecture is optimized for batch processing, which can lead to slower performance for certain real-time use cases. The write-heavy nature of HDFS can impact performance for applications that require frequent updates. Additionally, as the data landscape evolves, newer distributed file systems are emerging to address the limitations of existing solutions.

Distributed file systems like Hadoop HDFS have transformed how organizations manage and process data in the era of Big Data. By distributing data across multiple nodes and providing fault tolerance and scalability, HDFS has paved the way for efficient storage, retrieval, and processing of massive datasets. Its architecture and features make it a cornerstone of modern data infrastructure, supporting many use cases from batch processing to analytical insights. As data continues to increase and evolve, distributed file systems will remain critical in empowering Big Data workloads and driving innovations in data management and analysis.

Chapter IV

Data Preprocessing and Transformation

Data Cleaning and Imputation

In the realm of data-driven decision-making, the quality and integrity of data are paramount. However, the data collected from various sources is often plagued by errors, inconsistencies, and missing values. Data cleaning and imputation are essential processes that ensure the accuracy and reliability of data, enabling organizations to derive meaningful insights and make knowledgeable decisions. This section explores the significance of data cleaning and imputation, delves into the challenges and techniques involved, and underscores their role in shaping the foundation of trustworthy data analysis.

Data cleaning, also known as data cleansing or scrubbing, involves identifying and correcting errors, inconsistencies, and inaccuracies in datasets. The data collected from sources such as surveys, sensors, and databases can be riddled with typographical errors, duplicate entries, and missing values. These discrepancies can lead to faulty analyses and erroneous conclusions. Data cleaning aims to rectify these issues, ensuring that the data accurately represents the underlying reality and enabling researchers, analysts, and decision-makers to rely on the integrity of the data.

Data cleaning is not without challenges. The sheer volume of data generated today makes manual inspection and correction impractical. Automating the process requires robust algorithms that can identify anomalies and inconsistencies. The complexity of data further exacerbates the challenge. Data can be structured, semi-structured, or unstructured, containing text, images, and numerical values. Cleaning data spanning multiple formats demands versatile techniques to handle diverse data types.

Data cleaning employs a variety of techniques to rectify errors and inconsistencies. Deduplication identifies and removes duplicate records, ensuring that each entry is unique. Standardization harmonizes data by converting it into a consistent format, such as converting dates to a uniform layout. Validation checks data against predefined rules or constraints to detect outliers and anomalies. Transformation involves converting data into a suitable format, such as converting currency values to a common unit. Imputation, a crucial aspect of data cleaning, involves filling in missing values with estimated or predicted values.

Imputation is critical in data cleaning, especially when dealing with missing values. Missing data can arise for various reasons, such as survey non-response, system errors, or intentional omission. Imputation addresses the challenge of missing data by estimating and inserting values that are likely to reflect the true nature of the data. Imputation techniques range from simple methods like mean imputation, where missing values are replaced with the mean of the available values, to more complex processes such as regression imputation, which uses regression models to forecast missing values based on other variables.

While imputation enhances the completeness of datasets, it introduces the potential for bias if not executed carefully. Imputed values should be representative of the missing values to avoid distorting the analysis. Imputation methods should be chosen based on the data's characteristics and the analysis's goals. Additionally, imputation should be transparent and documented, allowing others to understand how missing values were addressed and ensuring the reproducibility of results.

Data cleaning and imputation play a vital role in data analysis and decision-making. The insights derived from cleaned and imputed data are more accurate and trustworthy, fostering confidence in the analysis outcomes. Decision-makers can rely on the results to guide strategies and actions. Furthermore, accurate and reliable data enhances the credibility of research studies, enabling the scientific community to draw valid conclusions and make meaningful contributions to knowledge.

Advancements in technology have revolutionized the landscape of data cleaning. Automated tools and software can identify and rectify errors at scale, reducing the reliance on manual efforts. Accurate and effective data cleaning is made possible by machine learning algorithms that may be trained to identify patterns of errors and inconsistencies. AI-powered solutions offer the potential to streamline the process and minimize human intervention, particularly in scenarios involving massive datasets.

Ethical considerations are paramount in the realm of data cleaning and imputation. Transparency is essential when applying data cleaning techniques, especially imputation, as the choices can significantly impact the results. Clear documentation of the methods, rationale, and potential implications ensures accountability and transparency. Additionally, ethical considerations extend to preserving data privacy and security, especially when sharing cleaned and imputed datasets.

Data cleaning and imputation are the guardians of data integrity in the age of information abundance. By identifying errors, inconsistencies, and missing values, these processes ensure that data accurately reflects reality, enabling organizations to make knowledgeable decisions and drive meaningful insights. As technology evolves, automated tools and AI-powered solutions will continue refining and expediting data cleaning. Ethical considerations will remain essential, ensuring that the choices made in data cleaning and imputation uphold transparency, accountability, and data privacy. Ultimately, data cleaning and imputation are not just technical processes; they support the credibility and trustworthiness of data analysis, shaping the foundation of a data-driven world.

Feature Selection and Engineering

In the landscape of machine learning and data analysis, the quality and relevance of features play a pivotal role in shaping the accuracy and effectiveness of predictive models. Feature selection and engineering are strategic processes that focus on identifying, selecting, and crafting the most informative features from raw data. These processes are essential for maximizing the performance of machine learning algorithms, enabling the extraction of meaningful patterns, and reducing the dimensionality of data. This section delves into the significance of feature selection and engineering, explores their techniques, and underscores their role in enhancing the efficiency and efficacy of data-driven solutions.

Features, also known as variables or attributes, are the building blocks of data representation. They encompass the characteristics, properties, or measurements that define each data point. The quality of features profoundly influences the performance of machine learning algorithms. Irrelevant, redundant, or noisy features can introduce noise and adversely affect model accuracy and generalization. Conversely, informative and discriminative features enable algorithms to discern patterns and relationships that lead to accurate predictions and insights.

The process of choosing a subset of the most pertinent and informative features from the initial set of variables is known as feature selection. The goal is to retain only those features that contribute significantly to the prediction task while discarding extraneous or redundant ones. Feature selection has several benefits, including reducing the risk of overfitting, improving model interpretability, and accelerating model training and prediction. Techniques for feature selection range from filter methods that rank features based on statistical metrics to wrapper methods that employ machine learning algorithms to evaluate feature subsets.

Feature engineering involves creating new features or transforming existing ones to enhance the predictive power of machine learning models. It requires domain knowledge and creativity to derive meaningful insights from the data. Feature engineering combines existing features, creates interaction terms, applies mathematical transformations, and incorporates domain-specific knowledge. For example, feature engineering might involve extracting text-based features like word frequency, sentiment scores, and linguistic patterns in natural language processing.

Feature engineering can potentially transform the data landscape and unlock hidden insights. It enables models to capture complex relationships that might not be apparent in the original data. By creating features that encapsulate domain knowledge or relevant contextual information, feature engineering empowers models to make accurate predictions and robust classifications. Moreover, feature engineering can address challenges related to data imbalance, missing values, and noisy features, enhancing the model's resilience to real-world data complexities.

Feature selection and engineering bridge the gap between domain knowledge and data analysis. Effective feature selection requires understanding the underlying domain and the context of the problem. Domain experts can identify features that are most relevant to the task at hand, ensuring that the selected features align with the analysis objectives. On the other hand, feature engineering demands creativity and a deep understanding of how data characteristics translate into informative features. A holistic approach that combines domain expertise and data manipulation skills is essential for successful feature selection and engineering.

Feature selection and engineering have a wide array of applications across diverse industries. In healthcare, predictive models can be built to diagnose diseases or predict patient outcomes using relevant medical features. In finance, models can utilize financial indicators and market data to forecast stock prices or detect fraudulent transactions. Natural language processing leverages feature engineering to extract linguistic features contributing to sentiment analysis or topic classification. Regardless of the domain, the effectiveness of machine learning models heavily relies on the quality of features and their representation of underlying patterns.

While feature selection and engineering offer substantial benefits, they are not without challenges. The curse of dimensionality, where the number of features exceeds the number of observations, can hinder model performance. Careful consideration is required to balance reducing dimensionality and retaining meaningful information. Overfitting is another challenge, as creating too many features or intricate transformations can result to models that execute well on training data but fail to generalize to new data.

Feature selection and engineering are the keys to unlocking the latent potential within data. By identifying informative features and crafting new ones, these processes empower machine learning algorithms to make accurate predictions, classifications, and insights. Effective feature selection enhances model interpretability and reduces computational complexity, while feature engineering enriches data representations, enabling models to capture intricate relationships. The interplay between domain knowledge, data manipulation skills, and machine learning expertise is critical for mastering feature selection and engineering. As organizations seek to extract valuable insights and drive innovation from data, the art of feature selection and engineering emerges as a cornerstone in the journey toward impactful data-driven solutions.

Dealing with Missing Data

In data analysis and decision-making, missing data is a common challenge that can significantly impact the quality and reliability of insights derived from datasets. Missing data can arise for various reasons, including survey non-response, data entry errors, and system failures. Addressing missing data is essential to ensure the accuracy and validity of analytical results. This section delves into the complexities of missing data, explores the strategies for handling it, and highlights the significance of these approaches in enhancing data quality and analysis.

Missing data poses a fundamental challenge in data analysis, as it disrupts the completeness and integrity of datasets. Ignoring missing data or treating it as insignificant can lead to biased and misleading results. The presence of missing data can impact the performance of statistical analyses, predictive models, and machine learning algorithms. Therefore, understanding the nature of missing data and employing appropriate strategies is crucial for accurate data-driven decision-making.

Missing data can be classified into three main types: missing completely at random (or MCAR), missing at random (or MAR), and missing not at random (or MNAR). MCAR refers to cases where the probability of data being missing is unrelated to the observed or unobserved values. MAR indicates that the probability of missing data depends on observed values, not unobserved ones. MNAR, on the other hand, indicates that the probability of missing data depends on observed and unobserved values. The type of missing data influences the choice of imputation methods and the potential for bias in analysis.

Imputation is a fundamental strategy for addressing missing data, involving estimating or predicting missing values based on available information. Imputation aims to create a complete dataset for analysis without introducing excessive bias or distorting the underlying patterns in the data. Various imputation methods exist, from simple techniques like mean imputation, where missing values are replaced with the mean of available values, to more advanced approaches like regression imputation and machine learning-based imputation.

Regression imputation leverages the relationships between variables to predict missing values. Linear regression models, for instance, can be trained using observed values as predictors to estimate missing values. This approach is effective when a significant correlation exists between the variable with missing data and other relevant variables. Regression imputation can produce accurate imputed values, but it assumes linearity and may not work well when relationships are nonlinear or complex.

Multiple imputation is a technique that addresses the uncertainty associated with imputed values. Instead of imputing a single value for each missing entry, multiple imputation generates multiple imputed datasets by introducing randomness into the imputation process. These datasets are then analyzed separately, and the results are combined to give a more accurate estimate of parameter estimates and their uncertainty. Multiple imputation is particularly useful when the missing data mechanism is not entirely understood.

Nonparametric imputation methods do not assume specific parametric relationships between variables. Instead, they rely on the inherent characteristics of the data to estimate missing values. For categorical data, mode imputation replaces missing values with the most frequent value in the dataset. For continuous data, imputation can be based on the median, which is less sensitive to outliers than the mean. Nonparametric methods are robust to violations of distributional assumptions and can provide reliable imputations in diverse data scenarios.

While imputation techniques offer a way to address missing data, they are not without challenges. Imputed values should reflect the plausible range of the variable and adhere to the relationships present in the data. Careful consideration is required to avoid introducing bias or creating artificial patterns through imputation. Moreover, imputation assumes that the missing data mechanism is known or can be reasonably inferred. If the missing data mechanism is unclear or nonignorable, the imputed values might not accurately reflect the true values.

Dealing with missing data is a critical aspect of data analysis that directly influences the accuracy and reliability of insights derived from datasets. The complexity of missing data requires a nuanced approach, considering the type of missing data, the relationships between variables, and the potential for bias. Imputation techniques offer effective strategies to fill in missing values and create complete datasets for analysis. Whether through regression imputation, multiple imputation, or nonparametric methods, the goal is to ensure that imputed values respect the characteristics of the data and enhance rather than distort the analysis outcomes.

Addressing missing data is not just a technical challenge but a fundamental aspect of data integrity and the foundation of trustworthy analysis. As organizations strive to make data-driven judgments and gain meaningful insights, the art of handling missing data emerges as an essential skill that elevates the quality and rigor of data analysis, ultimately completing the puzzle of understanding the complex relationships and patterns within the data.

Chapter V

Exploratory Data Analysis (EDA)

Importance of EDA in Data Science

Exploratory Data Analysis (EDA) serves as the compass that guides data scientists through the uncharted territory of raw datasets, uncovering patterns, insights, and nuances that drive informed decision-making. As the foundation of data science, EDA transforms data from mere numbers into meaningful narratives, bridging the gap between data and actionable insights. This section delves into the critical role of EDA in data science, explores its techniques and benefits, and highlights its significance in the process of extracting value from data.

EDA is the preliminary data analysis phase involving visual and statistical data exploration. It entails a systematic process of summarizing, visualizing, and comprehending the main characteristics of a dataset. EDA sets the stage for subsequent data modeling and hypothesis testing, offering a comprehensive view of the data's structure, distribution, relationships, and anomalies. This initial exploration provides context, identifies potential challenges, and shapes the direction of subsequent analyses.

Visualization is a cornerstone of EDA, offering a powerful means to depict data patterns and relationships. Visualizations transform raw data into intuitive representations that can be easily interpreted and understood. Scatter plots unveil the relationships between two variables, line charts reveal trends over time, and histograms display the data distribution. Box plots expose outliers and variations, while heatmaps unveil correlations across multiple variables. These visual cues enable data scientists to grasp complex interactions and identify noteworthy trends.

EDA uncovers essential statistics that provide insights into the data's central tendency and spread. Measures like the mean, median, and mode indicate the data's average or most common value. Standard deviation and variance reveal the extent of data dispersion around the mean. When coupled with visualizations, these statistics highlight data skewness, symmetry, and potential outliers. Such insights form the basis for informed decisions and hypothesis formulation.

Outliers, data points that substantially differ from the majority, can exert undue influence on statistical analyses and modeling outcomes. EDA helps identify and understand these anomalies, distinguishing between genuine outliers and data errors. Visualization tools like scatter plots and box plots reveal these deviations, enabling data scientists to decide whether to include, exclude, or transform these values. Addressing outliers in the EDA phase improves the accuracy and robustness of subsequent analyses.

In the modern era of Big Data, datasets often possess a high number of dimensions or variables. EDA plays a pivotal role in dimensionality reduction, helping data scientists identify redundant, irrelevant, or highly correlated variables. By eliminating or reducing the impact of such dimensions, EDA simplifies the data landscape, making it more manageable for subsequent modeling and analysis. Techniques like principal component analysis (PCA) leverage EDA insights to reduce the dimensionality while retaining meaningful information.

EDA lays the groundwork for data validation and preprocessing, critical steps that ensure data quality and consistency. EDA reveals missing values, inconsistencies, and data entry errors that can undermine analysis outcomes. These insights guide data scientists in making informed decisions about imputation techniques, data transformation, and handling missing data. Effective data preprocessing, built on the foundation of EDA, improves the accuracy and reliability of downstream analyses.

With technological advancements, interactive EDA tools empower data scientists to explore data dynamically. Interactive visualizations allow for real-time manipulation of data representations, facilitating the identification of trends, patterns, and outliers. Interactive dashboards enable users to tailor their exploration, fostering agile and iterative data analysis. These tools enhance the efficiency of EDA, enabling data scientists to delve deeper into data characteristics and relationships.

EDA is not a one-time process but an iterative journey that evolves as data insights unfold. The insights gained during EDA inform subsequent analyses, guiding the formulation of hypotheses, model selection, and experimental design. As data scientists progress through the analysis, new questions emerge, leading to further exploration and refinement of the EDA process. This iterative approach ensures the analysis remains data-driven and responsive to the insights revealed.

The real-world impact of EDA is palpable across diverse industries. In healthcare, EDA guides the discovery of patient trends, treatment efficacy, and disease patterns from medical records. In finance, EDA illuminates market trends, risk factors, and investment opportunities from complex financial datasets. EDA is indispensable in social sciences, uncovering demographic patterns, sentiment analysis, and behavioral trends from surveys and social media data. In each scenario, EDA catalyzes meaningful insights that drive informed decisions.

Exploratory Data Analysis is the gateway to understanding the nuances and narratives hidden within datasets. EDA transforms raw data into actionable insights by combining visualization, statistics, and domain knowledge. EDA sets the stage for accurate modeling, hypothesis testing, and informed decision-making. Its role in identifying patterns, relationships, and anomalies ensures data quality and integrity, enhancing the reliability of data-driven solutions. As data science continues to evolve, EDA remains a timeless and essential process that unveils the power of data, enabling organizations to harness its potential and drive meaningful impact.

Visualizing Data Distributions and Patterns

In data analysis, numbers often fail to convey the rich narratives hidden within datasets. Visualizing data distributions and patterns emerges as a transformative approach that transcends the confines of raw data, allowing complex relationships, trends, and anomalies to be intuitively grasped. This section delves into the significance of visualizing data distributions and patterns, explores various visualization techniques, and underscores the pivotal role of visualization in illuminating insights and driving informed decision-making.

Visualization is a language that bridges the gap between data and human cognition. It transforms abstract numerical values into visual representations that the human brain can interpret and understand. Visualizations leverage the brain's innate ability to process images, enabling complex data distributions and patterns to be grasped effortlessly. In a world inundated with data, visualization serves as the conduit through which insights emerge, enhancing the effectiveness of data analysis and communication.

Understanding the distribution of data is foundational to data analysis. Histograms, frequency plots, and density plots offer insights into the spread and concentration of data values. A symmetrical bell-shaped curve in a normal distribution reveals uniformity, while skewed distributions indicate concentration toward one side. Box plots provide a snapshot of data's central tendency, spread, and potential outliers. These visualizations enable analysts to discern patterns, identify deviations, and uncover data characteristics that inform subsequent analyses.

Visualizations unveil intricate relationships and trends that might remain hidden in raw data. Scatter plots, line charts, and heatmaps unveil correlations and associations between variables. Scatter plots showcase the relationships between two variables, allowing analysts to discern trends, clusters, or outliers. Line charts provide a visual narrative of trends over time or across categories. Heatmaps visualize patterns within matrices, revealing clusters or patterns that may not be apparent through numerical analysis alone.

Spatial data holds a unique position in visualization, offering insights into geographical relationships and distributions. Geographic information systems (GIS) and interactive maps enable analysts to explore spatial patterns, such as disease outbreaks, population density, and environmental factors. Spatial visualizations provide a holistic view of how data is distributed across regions, highlighting clusters, disparities, and potential spatial dependencies. These insights are invaluable in urban planning, epidemiology, and disaster response.

Time series data, characterized by data points collected over time, is prevalent in various domains, including finance, weather, and social media. Visualizing time series data through line and candlestick charts exposes temporal trends, cyclic patterns, and seasonality. These visualizations enable analysts to understand fluctuations, predict future trends, and uncover relationships between variables that evolve over time. Organizations can make well-informed decisions by using time series visualizations, which are based on past trends and projections for the future.

While visualization is a powerful tool, designing compelling visualizations requires careful consideration of data complexity and the audience's needs. Overloading a visualization with too much detail can overwhelm viewers, obscuring the insights it intends to convey. Striking a balance between complexity and clarity is essential to ensure the visualization resonates with the intended audience. Moreover, choosing appropriate visualization techniques that accurately represent the data's characteristics and relationships is crucial for conveying meaningful insights.

Advancements in technology have given rise to interactive visualizations that enable users to engage with data dynamically. Interactive dashboards, data exploration tools, and data storytelling platforms empower users to customize their exploration, drill down into specific data points, and quickly uncover insights. Interactive visualizations foster a sense of ownership and exploration, enabling users to ask questions, test hypotheses, and make discoveries in a self-guided manner.

Visualizing data distributions and patterns is not an end in itself; instead, it serves as a means to an end: informed decision-making. Visualizations provide the evidence and rationale needed to guide strategies, allocate resources, and devise solutions. Stakeholders across various domains, from business to healthcare to policy-making, rely on visualizations to communicate insights, align teams, and drive impactful actions. Visualizations transform data from abstract concepts into compelling narratives that catalyze change.

Visualization is a convergence of art and science, requiring analytical rigor and creative expression. Data scientists blend their expertise in data analysis with design principles to craft visualizations that are accurate, informative, and visually appealing. The choice of colors, layout, and visualization types influences how data is perceived and understood. Effective visualizations evoke emotions, prompt questions, and inspire deeper exploration, fostering a symbiotic relationship between data analysis and visual storytelling.

Visualizing data distributions and patterns is an art that transcends numbers and charts, allowing data to speak for itself. It is a process of revelation, transforming raw data into narratives that inspire understanding and action. Visualizations unravel complex relationships, uncover hidden insights, and enable stakeholders to make informed decisions. As organizations navigate the sea of data, visualization emerges as a guiding light, illuminating the paths that lead to meaningful insights and transformative impact. Visuals are a language that can express ideas more vividly than words, and a well-designed visualization can convey a thousand data points and enhance our comprehension of the world.

Identifying Outliers and Anomalies

Outliers and anomalies, those peculiar data points that deviate significantly from the norm, hold a unique position in data analysis.

Often dismissed as noise or errors, outliers and anomalies are, in fact, sources of rich insights that can uncover hidden patterns, uncover data quality issues, and guide decision-making. This section delves into the importance of identifying outliers and anomalies, explores the techniques used for detection, and highlights their role in enhancing data analysis and fostering accurate insights.

Outliers and anomalies are data points that lie far from the central tendency of a dataset. They can be attributed to various factors, including measurement errors, experimental noise, genuine data variations, or even exceptional events. While outliers are data points that diverge from the bulk of the data, anomalies refer to data points that exhibit unexpected behavior compared to the rest of the dataset. Detecting these exceptional data points is crucial for understanding the true nature of data, as they often signify underlying phenomena or issues that require attention.

Identifying outliers and anomalies is not just about data cleansing; it's about uncovering insights that might remain hidden in the presence of noise. Outliers can reveal meaningful relationships, trends, or phenomena that conventional analysis overlooks. Anomalies often warn early about fraud, errors, or system malfunctions. Identifying outliers also serves as a quality assessment tool, guaranteeing the accuracy and dependability of the data utilized in analysis.

Visualizations play a pivotal role in spotting outliers and anomalies. Box plots, scatter plots, and histograms visually highlight data points outside the expected range. Box plots provide a snapshot of the data's central tendency and spread, revealing potential outliers. Scatter plots expose the relationships between two variables, making outliers visually apparent. Histograms showcase the distribution of data and highlight tails that contain potential outliers. These visual cues empower analysts to discern patterns that guide further investigation.

Statistical methods are foundational in outlier detection, offering objective criteria to identify exceptional data points. Z-scores, calculated by measuring the number of standard deviations a data point is from the mean, help identify values that fall significantly far from the norm. Data points with high absolute Z-scores are potential outliers. Percentiles, mainly the interquartile range (IQR), provide a robust measure of spread resistant to outliers. Data points beyond a certain percentile threshold can be flagged as potential outliers.

Machine learning techniques have revolutionized outlier and anomaly detection by enabling the identification of complex patterns in high-dimensional datasets. Clustering algorithms like k-means and DBSCAN can separate outliers from the main clusters. Isolation Forest and One-Class SVM are explicitly designed for identifying outliers. These algorithms model the normal behavior of data and identify deviations as potential anomalies. Machine learning-based approaches are beneficial in scenarios where simple statistical measures do not easily define outliers.

Time series data introduces a unique challenge in detecting anomalies, as temporal relationships must be considered. Time series data can be analyzed by using techniques like exponential smoothing, moving averages, and seasonal decomposition to find trends and patterns. Deviations from these patterns indicate potential anomalies. Additionally, forecasting models can predict future values, and deviations from these predictions can signal anomalies or sudden changes in data behavior.

Identifying outliers and anomalies is not a one-size-fits-all process; it requires contextual understanding and domain expertise. What constitutes an outlier in one context might be a norm in another. Incorporating domain knowledge helps define the boundaries of normal behavior and guides the identification of exceptional data points. Understanding the data's context, characteristics, and the underlying processes that generate it is essential for accurate detection.

While outlier and anomaly detection offer significant benefits, challenges arise in distinguishing true anomalies from noise or natural variations. The choice of detection methods and parameters can influence the number of flagged outliers. Interpreting the significance of identified outliers requires careful consideration of the data's context and the potential impact of these anomalies on analysis outcomes. Misinterpreting anomalies can lead to erroneous conclusions and misguided actions.

Identifying outliers and anomalies plays a crucial role in decision-making across various domains. In finance, outliers can signal potential fraud or market abnormalities. In healthcare, anomalies can detect disease outbreaks or patient outliers. In manufacturing, identifying anomalies can prevent product defects or equipment failures. By recognizing exceptional data points, organizations can make informed decisions, allocate resources effectively, and mitigate risks before they escalate.

Outliers and anomalies are the outliers that deserve special attention. Rather than disregarding them as noise, data analysts and scientists should embrace their potential to reveal hidden insights, uncover patterns, and flag issues. Detecting outliers is an iterative process that combines statistical rigor, domain knowledge, and contextual understanding. Machine learning techniques improve the capacity to recognize intricate patterns and relationships in data as technology develops. Organizations can use outliers and anomalies to inform decisions, improve data quality, and reveal the stories hidden beyond the surface of raw data by illuminating extraordinary data values.

Chapter VI

Machine Learning Fundamentals

Introduction to Supervised, Unsupervised, and Semi-Supervised Learning

Machine learning, a cornerstone of artificial intelligence, encompasses diverse methodologies that enable computers to learn from data and make predictions or decisions. Within the realm of machine learning, three fundamental paradigms stand out: supervised learning, unsupervised learning, and semi-supervised learning. Each paradigm addresses distinct challenges and scenarios, catering to the multifaceted nature of data analysis and prediction. This section explores these paradigms' core concepts and applications, illuminating their significance in driving advancements in various fields.

Supervised learning is the most prevalent and intuitive paradigm in machine learning. It entails using labeled data to train a model, where each input instance has a matching output label. Finding an input-to-output mapping that is well-suited to new, untested data is the goal. Typical supervised learning tasks include regression, in which the model predicts continuous values, and classification, in which the model labels inputs from a specified set. Supervised learning algorithms, which are effective tools for predictive modeling, learn from the relationship between inputs and outputs. Examples of these algorithms include decision trees, support vector machines, and neural networks.

Supervised learning finds applications in numerous domains: healthcare, finance, e-commerce, and more. In medical diagnosis, models can learn to predict diseases based on patient data, assisting doctors in making informed decisions. Recommender systems employ supervised learning to suggest products, movies, or music based on user preferences and historical interactions. In finance, models predict stock prices, detect fraudulent transactions, and assess credit risk. The cornerstone of supervised learning lies in its reliance on labeled data, which serves as a roadmap for the model to learn patterns and relationships inherent in the data.

Unsupervised learning shifts the focus from labeled data to unlabeled data, aiming to discover underlying patterns, structures, and relationships within the data. In this paradigm, the model explores the data without predefined output labels, clustering similar data points together or reducing the dimensionality of data. Clustering algorithms, like k-means and hierarchical clustering, group similar data points, while dimensionality reduction techniques like principal component analysis (PCA) capture the most essential features of the data. Unsupervised learning is beneficial for exploratory data analysis and data preprocessing.

Unsupervised learning has a wide array of applications across industries. In market segmentation, businesses use clustering algorithms to categorize customers into distinct segments based on their behaviors or preferences. Natural language processing leverages unsupervised learning for topic modeling, where documents are grouped based on the topics they discuss. Anomaly detection is another domain where unsupervised learning shines, identifying outliers or unusual patterns in data. Unsupervised learning helps analysts uncover hidden structures and relationships that may not be apparent in labeled data, making it a valuable tool for gaining insights into complex datasets.

Semi-supervised learning lies in the middle between supervised and the unsupervised learning. It combines the strengths of both paradigms by using a small amount of labeled data alongside a larger amount of unlabeled data. The labeled data guides the model, while the unlabeled data aids in capturing the underlying structure. Semi-supervised learning is beneficial when obtaining large amounts of labeled data is expensive or time-consuming. Many real-world scenarios fall into this category, making semi-supervised learning a practical approach to leveraging the benefits of labeled and unlabeled data.

Semi-supervised learning has found applications in various domains, including natural language processing and computer vision. In machine translation, models can be trained on a combination of translated sentences (labeled data) and monolingual sentences (unlabeled data), improving translation quality. Speech recognition systems benefit from semi-supervised learning by utilizing transcribed speech data (labeled) and untranscribed speech data (unlabeled) to enhance accuracy. The beauty of semi-supervised learning lies in its adaptability to real-world scenarios where labeled data is limited but valuable insights can still be gleaned from the abundance of unlabeled data.

Supervised, unsupervised, and semi-supervised learning form a spectrum of machine learning paradigms that collectively cater to various challenges. Labeled data is abundant in some cases, making supervised learning the go-to choice for predictive modeling. Unsupervised learning uncovers underlying structures and relationships in scenarios where labels are scarce or unavailable. Semi-supervised learning bridges the gap by harnessing labeled and unlabeled data, making it a valuable approach in scenarios between the extremes of labeled and unlabeled data availability.

The trio of supervised, unsupervised, and semi-supervised learning exemplifies the versatility of machine learning, accommodating diverse data types, volumes, and objectives. These paradigms collectively empower data scientists and machine learning practitioners to explore, understand, and extract insights from data in many contexts. Whether it's making accurate predictions, uncovering hidden patterns, or efficiently leveraging limited labeled data, the spectrum of machine learning paradigms stands as a testament to the dynamism and ingenuity of modern data analysis and predictive modeling. As the field continues to evolve, these paradigms will continue to be the cornerstone of innovation and discovery in machine learning.

Regression and Classification Algorithms

Regression and classification algorithms are pillars of machine learning, empowering data scientists to make predictions and decisions based on data patterns. These algorithms enable extracting valuable insights from datasets, transforming raw data into actionable information. While regression algorithms predict continuous outcomes, classification algorithms assign labels to data points. This section delves into the core concepts of regression and classification, explores representative algorithms, and highlights their applications in diverse domains.

Regression algorithms serve as the bedrock of predictive modeling when the objective is to estimate a continuous target variable based on input features. These algorithms capture the relationships between variables, enabling the predicting of future outcomes. Linear regression, a fundamental technique, models the relationship as a straight line, intending to minimize the difference between predicted and actual values. Polynomial regression extends this concept by fitting higher-degree polynomials to data, accommodating nonlinear relationships.

Regression algorithms find applications in numerous domains, shaping decision-making processes. In economics, regression models forecast market trends and estimate demand for products. Healthcare leverages regression to predict patient outcomes, understand disease progression, and assess treatment efficacy. Environmental studies employ regression to model the impact of variables like pollution or temperature on ecosystems. The versatility of regression algorithms empowers analysts to uncover relationships, quantify effects, and make informed predictions in a wide range of scenarios.

Classification algorithms tackle problems where the goal is to assign categorical labels to data points based on their features. These algorithms learn decision boundaries that partition the feature space into distinct regions corresponding to different classes. Logistic regression, as the name suggests, is a classification technique that calculates the likelihood that an instance falls into a specific class. Decision trees recursively partition data based on feature values, while support vector machines optimize a hyperplane that best separates classes.

Classification algorithms play a pivotal role in solving real-world challenges across industries. Medical diagnosis distinguishes between healthy and diseased patients based on medical data. Image recognition applications, like the facial recognition and object detection, utilize classification algorithms to identify and label objects within images. Fraud detection in finance employs classification to flag suspicious transactions. Classification algorithms provide the tools to automate decision-making processes, optimize resource allocation, and enhance accuracy in many contexts.

Ensemble methods combine multiple regression or classification models to improve predictive performance. Bagging and boosting are prominent ensemble techniques. Random Forest, a bagging approach, constructs an ensemble of decision trees trained on bootstrapped data samples. Gradient Boosting, a boosting technique, iteratively builds models that correct errors of previous models. Ensemble methods mitigate overfitting, enhance generalization, and amplify the predictive power of individual models.

Modern machine learning libraries and tools provide accessible platforms for implementing regression and classification algorithms. Scikit-learn, a popular Python library, offers various algorithms, from linear regression to support vector machines. TensorFlow and PyTorch, deep learning frameworks, enable the implementation of complex neural network architectures for both regression and classification tasks. These tools streamline the implementation process, democratizing machine learning and fostering innovation across domains.

Selecting the appropriate regression or classification algorithm depends on the data's characteristics, problem requirements, and computational resources. Linear regression suits simple relationships, while decision trees handle nonlinear patterns well. Deep learning models excel at complex tasks like image recognition but may require substantial computational power. The data's size, dimensionality, and noise levels also influence algorithm selection. The iterative process of experimentation and evaluation aids in identifying the best-performing algorithm for a given problem.

Regression and classification algorithms form the cornerstone of predictive modeling and decision-making in machine learning. These algorithms enable data scientists to extract insights, make predictions, and automate decision processes across diverse domains. By harnessing the relationships between variables and learning decision boundaries, regression and classification algorithms amplify the value of data, transforming it into actionable information. As machine learning continues to evolve, these algorithms will remain fundamental tools that empower analysts, scientists, and practitioners to navigate the complexities of data analysis and drive innovation in the digital age.

Clustering and Dimensionality Reduction Techniques

Clustering and dimensionality reduction are essential techniques in data analysis and machine learning, serving as powerful tools to uncover hidden patterns, simplify complex data, and enhance the efficiency of subsequent analyses. Clustering techniques group similar data points together, revealing underlying structures, while dimensionality reduction methods condense high-dimensional data into a more manageable form without losing critical information. This section explores the significance of clustering and dimensionality reduction, delves into representative techniques, and highlights their role in extracting insights from data.

Clustering techniques partition data into groups, or clusters, based on the similarity of data points. These techniques enable the identification of inherent structures and relationships within datasets. K-means clustering is a widely utilized method that assigns data points to clusters by reducing the distances between points and the cluster centroids. Hierarchical clustering constructs a tree-like structure of clusters, facilitating the exploration of different granularity levels. Density-based methods like DBSCAN identify clusters based on the density of data points, suitable for datasets with irregular shapes and noise.

Clustering techniques find applications in various domains, driving insights and decision-making. In marketing, customer segmentation identifies groups of similar customers for targeted campaigns. Image analysis employs clustering to group similar regions in images, enabling object detection and image compression. Genetics benefits from clustering by identifying distinct genetic profiles for disease classification. Clustering techniques unravel patterns that can be leveraged for understanding, optimization, and resource allocation across diverse industries.

Dimensionality reduction techniques tackle the "curse of dimensionality," a challenge arising when datasets possess numerous features. High-dimensional data is prone to sparsity, computational complexity, and overfitting. Principal Component Analysis (or PCA) is a prominent technique that transforms data into a lower-dimensional space while preserving as much variance as possible. t-SNE (t-Distributed Stochastic Neighbor Embedding) focuses on preserving the pairwise similarities between data points, making it suitable for visualizing high-dimensional data in lower dimensions.

Dimensionality reduction techniques have diverse applications that span visualization, noise reduction, and preprocessing. In data visualization, dimensionality reduction projects high-dimensional data into two or three dimensions to preserve the most informative aspects. Feature selection, a subset of dimensionality reduction, identifies the most relevant features, improving model interpretability and efficiency. Noise reduction enhances data quality by eliminating irrelevant features that may introduce noise and distort patterns.

Combining clustering and dimensionality reduction techniques creates a synergy that amplifies insights. Before applying clustering algorithms, dimensionality reduction can simplify high-dimensional data, making the clustering process computationally efficient and mitigating the "curse of dimensionality." The reduced-dimension representation can capture the most salient aspects of data, ensuring that clustering algorithms capture meaningful relationships. This synergy enhances the interpretability and effectiveness of both techniques.

Implementing clustering and dimensionality reduction techniques has become more accessible due to the availability of machine learning libraries and tools. Scikit-learn, a popular Python library, offers many clustering algorithms, including K-means and hierarchical clustering. The same library provides PCA and t-SNE implementations for dimensionality reduction. These tools democratize the adoption of these techniques, enabling data scientists to integrate them into their analyses seamlessly.

Selecting the appropriate clustering or dimensionality reduction technique depends on the data's characteristics, objectives, and computational constraints. The number of clusters or dimensions to retain can impact results significantly. Understanding the trade-offs between preserving information and reducing complexity is crucial.

Exploratory analysis and experimentation guide the choice of technique, allowing data scientists to identify the methods that best align with their objectives.

Clustering and dimensionality reduction techniques are cornerstones of data analysis that unlock insights and streamline the analytical process. Clustering uncovers hidden structures within data, enabling pattern recognition and resource optimization. Dimensionality reduction simplifies high-dimensional data, enhancing efficiency and mitigating challenges posed by the curse of dimensionality. When used in conjunction, these techniques amplify their individual capabilities, yielding more profound insights into complex datasets. As data analysis landscape continues to evolve, clustering and dimensionality reduction remain indispensable tools that empower analysts, scientists, and practitioners to navigate the intricacies of data, extract valuable insights, and drive innovation in a data-rich world.

Chapter VII

Big Data Analytics
with Machine Learning

Challenges and Opportunities in Applying ML to Big Data

The fusion of machine learning (ML) with big data has ushered in a new era of possibilities, enabling organizations to derive unprecedented insights and drive innovation. However, the marriage of these two powerful technologies brings with it a unique set of challenges and opportunities. This section delves into the intricacies of applying machine learning to big data, highlighting the inherent challenges and the potential opportunities for organizations to harness the full potential of this dynamic partnership.

Big data, characterized by its volume, velocity, variety, and veracity, offers vast opportunities for organizations willing to harness its potential. The vast amount of data produced by multiple platforms, such as social media, sensors, and transactions, offers a plethora of knowledge that is just waiting to be discovered. Real-time data streams, driven by the rapid pace of technological advancement, allow for timely insights and actions. The diversity of data types, from structured to unstructured, presents an opportunity to explore previously untapped sources of knowledge. Additionally, the integrity of data introduces the need for advanced techniques that ensure the accuracy and reliability of insights. As organizations embrace the challenges of big data, they simultaneously embrace a realm of opportunities that can reshape industries, optimize operations, and drive strategic decision-making.

While big data opens doors to insights, the sheer variety and volume of data pose substantial challenges. Traditional data management systems struggle to handle the scale and diversity of big data. Unstructured data, such as text and images, requires specialized techniques for extraction and analysis. Moreover, the velocity at which data is generated demands real-time processing capabilities. Distributed computing frameworks like Hadoop and Spark have emerged to address these challenges, offering scalable solutions for processing and analyzing big data. However, effectively managing the complexity of data variety and volume requires a concerted effort in data integration, preprocessing, and infrastructure development.

The veracity of big data raises concerns about data quality and reliability. Data streaming in from various sources amplifies the potential for errors, inconsistencies, and inaccuracies. Inaccurate data can lead to erroneous conclusions and misguided decisions. Ensuring data quality requires thorough data cleaning, validation, and quality control processes. Advanced techniques, such as anomaly detection and outlier analysis, help identify and rectify data irregularities. The challenge lies in establishing robust data governance practices that ensure the veracity of insights derived from big data, fostering trust in the outcomes and guiding sound decision-making.

The velocity of data in the big data ecosystem necessitates scalable solutions that can process and analyze data in real time. Traditional ML algorithms designed for smaller datasets may struggle to meet the demands of big data analysis. Scalable ML techniques, such as distributed training and parallel processing, address this challenge by enabling algorithms to scale across clusters of machines. Leveraging cloud computing infrastructure allows organizations to scale resources according to computational demands. By navigating scalability and performance challenges, organizations can harness the full potential of big data-driven ML and unlock insights faster than ever before.

As organizations delve into the world of big data, they must navigate the ethical complexities surrounding data privacy and security. With access to vast amounts of personal information, there is a risk of violating user privacy and compromising sensitive data. Regulatory frameworks, such as GDPR and HIPAA, impose stringent requirements for the responsible handling of personal data. Differential privacy techniques and data anonymization methods help mitigate privacy risks while still allowing for valuable analysis. Ethical considerations, transparency, and informed consent become paramount as organizations strive to balance the benefits of big data with the protection of individual rights and societal well-being.

Amidst the challenges, ML and big data convergence presents transformative opportunities across industries. In healthcare, predictive analytics on patient data can drive personalized treatments and improve medical outcomes. In finance, ML models analyze vast amounts of transaction data to detect real-time fraudulent activities. Through predictive maintenance and demand forecasting, manufacturing can optimize production processes and supply chains. The potential for innovations is limitless, ranging from smart cities and autonomous vehicles to precision agriculture and beyond. The key lies in leveraging big data-driven ML to solve complex problems and reshape industries for the better.

Addressing the challenges and opportunities of applying ML to big data requires an interdisciplinary approach. Data scientists, domain experts, data engineers, and ethicists must collaborate to ensure that the full potential of big data-driven ML is realized while upholding ethical standards. Cross-functional teams are essential for designing effective ML models, developing robust data pipelines, and navigating data use's legal and ethical implications. This collaboration fosters holistic solutions that consider both technical and societal aspects, leading to responsible innovation.

Integrating machine learning and big data is a journey laden with challenges and rich with opportunities. By recognizing the intricacies of data variety, volume, quality, and privacy, organizations can navigate the complexities and harness the transformative potential of big data-driven ML. Ethical considerations, scalability, and interdisciplinary collaboration play crucial roles in shaping the trajectory of this journey. As organizations embrace the challenges head-on, they also embrace the prospect of reshaping industries, advancing knowledge, and driving positive change through the power of machine learning applied to big data.

Scalable Machine Learning Algorithms (e.g., MapReduce)

The digital age has led to an explosion in data, which has increased the need for scalable machine learning algorithms that can effectively process large volumes of data. As datasets grow exponentially, traditional algorithms struggle to meet computational demands. Enter MapReduce, a groundbreaking programming model that revolutionized the landscape of large-scale data processing and enabled the development of scalable machine learning algorithms. This section explores the significance of scalability in machine learning, delves into the mechanics of MapReduce, and showcases its applications in creating efficient, large-scale machine learning solutions.

The era of big data has ushered in unprecedented opportunities and challenges. Organizations across industries generate massive volumes of data, encompassing customer interactions, sensor readings, social media posts, and more. Traditional algorithms, optimized for smaller datasets, struggle to process and analyze this deluge of information efficiently. Scalable machine learning algorithms are imperative to tackle these challenges, offering the ability to process data at a larger scale without sacrificing performance or accuracy. In this context, scalability refers to the capability of algorithms to handle increasing data sizes, enabling insights from massive datasets in a reasonable amount of time.

MapReduce, initially introduced by Google and popularized by Apache Hadoop, is a programming model designed to process and analyze large datasets across distributed clusters of computers. The model divides data processing into two stages: the Map phase and the Reduce phase. In the Map phase, data is divided into smaller chunks, and a map function is applied to each chunk in parallel. In the Reduce phase, the results from the map phase are aggregated and combined to produce the final output. With MapReduce, developers may concentrate on designing algorithms instead of worrying about distributed computing difficulties, as the framework takes care of execution, distribution, and fault tolerance.

MapReduce has found widespread applications in creating scalable machine learning algorithms. Techniques like logistic regression, decision trees, and k-means clustering have been adapted to the MapReduce paradigm in model training. Large datasets are divided into segments, and computations are performed in parallel across the distributed cluster. The results are then aggregated to update model parameters. Beyond model training, MapReduce is employed in feature selection, dimensionality reduction, and anomaly detection, among other tasks. Its ability to process data in a distributed manner makes it a valuable tool in accelerating the development of large-scale machine learning solutions.

While MapReduce addresses scalability challenges, it introduces certain complexities and trade-offs. Not all algorithms can be easily adapted to the MapReduce paradigm, as some require iterative updates or shared states, which do not align with the model's design. Furthermore, the overhead associated with data distribution and aggregation can impact performance, especially for smaller datasets that may not fully utilize the distributed nature of the framework. Balancing the performance gains from parallel processing with the overhead introduced by MapReduce requires careful consideration and algorithm design.

While MapReduce played a pivotal role in advancing scalable machine learning, the landscape has evolved with the emergence of more sophisticated frameworks and platforms. Apache Spark, for example, provides faster in-memory processing compared to Hadoop's disk-based approach, making it well-suited for iterative machine learning algorithms. Cloud computing platforms like AWS (Amazon Web Services) and Microsoft Azure offer scalable infrastructure for running machine learning workloads without managing underlying clusters. These advancements expand the possibilities of scalable machine learning, allowing organizations to choose the framework that best aligns with their requirements.

The impact of scalable machine learning algorithms, powered by paradigms like MapReduce, extends across various domains. These algorithms are used in finance to analyze enormous volumes of transaction data and quickly identify fraudulent activity. Scalable machine learning is used by e-commerce sites to make product recommendations to users according to their browsing history and interests. Healthcare organizations analyze patient data to predict disease outcomes and personalize treatment plans. The scalability of these algorithms empowers data-driven decision-making, optimizes processes, and enhances customer experiences on a massive scale.

Scalable machine learning algorithms, propelled by paradigms like MapReduce, are the cornerstone of data analysis and insights in the age of big data. As the volume of data grows, the ability to process and analyze information efficiently becomes paramount. MapReduce's distributed computing model revolutionized how large-scale data processing is approached, enabling the development of algorithms that can handle massive datasets without sacrificing performance. While challenges and trade-offs exist, the advancements in scalable frameworks and platforms continue to refine the landscape, offering organizations the flexibility to choose the tools that align with their needs. As the journey of scalable machine learning continues, the horizons of possibilities expand, opening new avenues for innovation, discovery, and transformative insights from the vast sea of data.

Distributed Training and Model Deployment

The exponential growth of data and the increasing complexity of machine learning models have ushered in the need for distributed training and model deployment. Traditional approaches to training and deploying machine learning models struggle to keep up with the demands of large datasets and intricate model architectures. Distributed training harnesses the computational power of clusters to expedite training processes, while model deployment ensures that trained models are operational and accessible to make real-time predictions. This section delves into the significance of distributed training and model deployment, explores their mechanics, and highlights their impact on the scalability and effectiveness of machine learning systems.

Intricate model architectures, deep neural networks, and massive datasets characterize the era of modern machine learning. While these advancements have enabled breakthroughs in various fields, they also pose challenges related to training times, computational resources, and deployment efficiency. Traditional training processes that rely on single machines struggle to accommodate the computational demands of complex models and large datasets. Distributed training emerges as a solution to expedite training times and optimize resource utilization, paving the way for developing more powerful machine learning systems.

Distributed training involves the parallel execution of training processes across a cluster of interconnected machines. This approach leverages the combined computational power of multiple machines to accelerate the training of machine learning models. After the training data is split up into smaller batches, each batch is processed separately on multiple machines. The model parameters are updated in parallel, and the results are aggregated to refine the model. Distributed training frameworks like TensorFlow, PyTorch, and Horovod provide tools and APIs that facilitate the seamless distribution of computation across clusters.

The benefits of distributed training are manifold. One of the primary advantages is speed. Distributed training drastically reduces training times, enabling data scientists to rapidly iterate and experiment with model architectures. Moreover, as datasets grow in size, distributed training ensures that computations can be efficiently executed in parallel, making optimal use of available resources. Scalability is another key benefit, as distributed training frameworks can seamlessly scale to accommodate clusters of varying sizes, from a few machines to thousands.

While distributed training offers significant advantages, it introduces challenges related to communication and synchronization. The need for frequent communication and synchronization between machines can lead to network bottlenecks, slowing down the training process. Efficient data distribution, load balancing, and synchronization strategies are crucial to mitigate these challenges. Additionally, hardware heterogeneity across machines can impact performance, necessitating careful resource allocation and optimization.

Deploying a machine learning model for real-time prediction is a crucial step after it has been trained. Model deployment involves making the trained model operational and accessible to users or applications. Deployed models are integrated into production systems, enabling them to process incoming data and provide real-time predictions. The deployment process involves choosing the right infrastructure, managing scalability, monitoring model performance, and ensuring security.

Model deployment presents its own set of challenges. Ensuring consistency between the development and production environments is essential to avoid discrepancies that could lead to unexpected behavior. Continuous monitoring is crucial to track the model's performance over time and detect any degradation in prediction accuracy. Scalability is another consideration, as deployed models must handle varying levels of traffic and requests efficiently.

Distributed training and model deployment collectively amplify the scalability and efficiency of machine learning systems. Distributed training accelerates model development and optimization, enabling data scientists to explore a broader range of model architectures and hyperparameters. This accelerated development cycle translates into faster time-to-market for machine learning applications. Model deployment ensures that the fruits of training efforts are seamlessly integrated into operational systems, enabling real-time predictions and driving data-driven decision-making.

The impact of distributed training and model deployment reverberates across various industries. In autonomous vehicles, distributed training facilitates the development of robust perception and decision-making models. Healthcare benefits from real-time predictions for disease diagnosis and patient monitoring. E-commerce platforms leverage deployed models to personalize recommendations for customers. These applications illustrate how the synergy between distributed training and model deployment drives innovation and revolutionizes industries.

Distributed training and model deployment represent pivotal advancements in machine learning, addressing the challenges posed by complex models and large datasets. Distributed training accelerates model development, optimizing resource utilization and enabling rapid experimentation. Model deployment bridges the gap between training and inference, ensuring trained models deliver real-time predictions and insights to end-users. By harnessing the power of distributed computing and operationalizing trained models, organizations unlock the full potential of machine learning, transforming industries, enhancing decision-making, and driving innovation in the age of data.

Chapter VIII

Deep Learning
and Neural Networks

Basics of Neural Networks and Deep Learning

Deep learning and neural networks have become revolutionary technologies that propel artificial intelligence forward and allow machines to learn from and make judgments based on data. Rooted in the concept of simulating the human brain's neural structure, neural networks are the building blocks of deep learning architectures. This section delves into the fundamentals of neural networks and deep learning, exploring their structure, components, training process, and role in shaping the AI-driven solutions' landscape.

Neural networks draw inspiration from the human brain's intricate network of interconnected neurons. Each neuron processes input signals, applies weights to them, and generates an output signal. Neural networks replicate this process through layers of interlinked nodes, or artificial neurons. The perceptron, which consists of an input and an output layer, is the most basic type of neural network. More complex architectures, such as multi-layer perceptrons

(MLPs) and convolutional neural networks (CNNs), add hidden layers that enable the network to capture intricate patterns and features in data.

The central components of a neural network are its neurons, which process incoming data and send signals to the layer above. A weight is applied to each neuronal connection, which establishes the significance of the incoming signal. The network gains non-linearity via activation functions, which enables it to recognize intricate links in data. Tanh, ReLU (Rectified Linear Unit), and sigmoid are examples of common activation functions. Throughout training, the network learns the weights and biases associated with each neuron and modifies them to minimize the discrepancy between expected and actual results.

Training neural networks involves adjusting the weights and biases to minimize the prediction error, often quantified using a loss function. Backpropagation, an essential technique, calculates the gradient of the loss function concerning the model's parameters. The parameters are then updated using gradient descent in the gradient's opposite direction, progressively lowering the loss. This iterative process fine-tunes the network's parameters, allowing it to learn and generalize from the training data.

Deep learning takes neural networks to the next level by introducing depth through multiple hidden layers. These layers allow the network to capture intricate and hierarchical features in data. Deep learning architectures include CNNs for image analysis, recurrent neural networks (or RNNs) for sequential data, and transformer architectures for natural language processing. The depth of these architectures enables them to excel in tasks like image recognition, language translation, and speech synthesis.

The utilizations of neural networks and deep learning span various industries and domains. Deep learning models analyze medical images in healthcare to diagnose diseases and predict patient outcomes. They process massive datasets in finance to detect fraudulent transactions and predict market trends. Autonomous vehicles leverage neural networks to make real-time decisions based on sensor data. Language models like GPT-3 generate human-like text, revolutionizing content creation and natural language understanding.

While neural networks and deep learning have demonstrated remarkable achievements, they also present challenges. Data quality and quantity are crucial in the network's performance. The complexity of deep architectures can lead to overfitting, where the model learns noise in the data instead of general patterns. Interpreting the decisions of deep learning models remains a challenge, as their internal workings are often seen as "black boxes." Efforts to enhance interpretability and ethical considerations are ongoing areas of research.

Deep learning demands significant computational resources, especially with complex architectures and large datasets. Training deep networks can be time-consuming and requires access to powerful hardware, such as GPUs and TPUs, to accelerate computations. Cloud computing platforms provide scalable infrastructure for training and deploying deep learning models, democratizing access to resources for researchers and practitioners.

Artificial intelligence has undergone a revolution due to deep learning and neural networks, which allow machines to recognize complicated patterns and make judgments based on data. By emulating the brain's neural structure, neural networks process data through interconnected layers of artificial neurons. Deep learning architectures take this concept further by adding depth through multiple hidden layers, enabling the capture of intricate features. From healthcare to finance, neural networks and deep learning applications are reshaping industries and advancing AI solutions. As researchers continue to address challenges related to data, complexity, and interpretability, the journey of neural networks and deep learning propels the frontiers of AI, unlocking new possibilities and pushing the boundaries of what machines can achieve.

Convolutional Neural Networks (CNNs) for Image Data

With their revolutionary impact on the fields of image processing and visual recognition, convolutional neural networks, or CNNs, have become a key component of contemporary artificial intelligence. CNNs, which are deeply rooted in the complex processes of the human visual system, are remarkably effective in automatically learning and extracting complex properties from images, allowing computers to process, categorize, and interpret visual data. This section delves into the foundations of CNNs, explores their architecture, training process, and applications, and highlights their role in advancing the frontiers of image data analysis.

Images, as rich sources of information, pose unique challenges for machines to decipher. Unlike structured data, images consist of pixels arranged in a grid, and extracting meaningful features from raw pixel values requires sophisticated techniques. CNNs address this challenge by mimicking the human visual system's hierarchical approach to recognizing patterns and structures. Through a series of interconnected layers, CNNs learn to identify edges, textures, shapes, and objects, ultimately enabling machines to understand the content of images.

The architecture of CNNs is characterized by layers that sequentially process and transform input data. The fundamental building blocks are convolutional layers, which employ filters (also known as kernels) to scan the input image and extract specific features. These features are captured in feature maps, which represent the presence of particular patterns in the image. Subsequent layers, such as pooling and fully connected layers, refine the extracted features and make predictions based on them.

The training process of CNNs involves the iterative adjustment of the filters' weights to optimize the network's performance. During training, the network is fed with labeled data, and the loss function quantifies the difference between predicted and actual outcomes. Backpropagation computes gradients that indicate the direction in which the filter weights should be updated to minimize the loss. Optimization algorithms like the stochastic gradient descent (or

SGD) are employed to gradually update the weights, improving the network's ability to recognize features.

The essence of CNNs lies in their ability to leverage convolution and pooling operations to capture local patterns while reducing computational complexity. Convolution involves sliding filters across the input image to compute dot products and create feature maps. This operation catches spatial hierarchies of features. Pooling, however, downsamples the feature maps, preserving essential information while reducing the dimensionality. These operations enable CNNs to recognize intricate patterns and structures in images efficiently.

CNNs have catalyzed transformative applications across diverse industries. In image classification, CNNs can distinguish between different objects, animals, or human expressions in images. Object detection enables the identification and localization of multiple objects within an image, paving the way for autonomous vehicles and surveillance systems. CNNs are also at the heart of facial recognition systems, medical image analysis for disease diagnosis, and artistic style transfer that combines one image's features with another's style.

CNNs can be resource-intensive to train, mainly when working with limited data or computational resources. Transfer learning comes to the rescue by utilizing pretrained models that have learned features from large datasets. These pretrained models can be fine-tuned on domain-specific data to adapt their learned features to a particular task. This approach accelerates model development, boosts performance, and democratizes the adoption of CNNs for various applications.

Despite their remarkable achievements, CNNs have challenges. One significant concern is interpretability—understanding how and why a CNN makes a particular decision. The complex hierarchies of features learned by CNNs can make it challenging to discern the rationale behind their predictions. Ensuring that CNNs generalize well to unseen data is another challenge, as overfitting to training data can limit their real-world applicability.

Convolutional Neural Networks (CNNs) stand as a testament to the remarkable capabilities of artificial intelligence to comprehend and interpret visual data. By emulating the human visual system's hierarchical processing, CNNs revolutionize image analysis, enabling machines to learn and recognize intricate patterns from raw pixel values. From image classification and object detection to medical diagnostics and artistic creations, the applications of CNNs span many domains, transforming industries and driving innovation. As the journey of CNNs continues, addressing challenges in interpretability and generalization paves the way for pioneering visual intelligence that transcends the boundaries of human perception and propels the field of artificial intelligence into uncharted territories.

Recurrent Neural Networks (RNNs) for Sequential Data

In artificial intelligence, understanding and predicting data sequences is a fundamental challenge with diverse applications. Enter Recurrent Neural Networks (RNNs), a class of neural networks specially designed to handle sequential data by incorporating the element of time. RNNs have transformed the landscape of natural language processing, time series analysis, and beyond by enabling machines to grasp the temporal dependencies inherent in sequences. This section delves into the mechanics of RNNs, explores their architecture, training process, and real-world applications, and highlights their role in shaping the future of temporal modeling.

Sequences are intrinsic to numerous domains—speech, text, music, stock prices, etc. Analyzing and predicting sequences requires an understanding of the temporal relationships between elements. Traditional machine learning models often struggle to capture these temporal dependencies, as they treat input data as isolated instances. RNNs address this limitation by introducing memory mechanisms that enable the network to retain information about previous elements in the sequence and incorporate it into the analysis of subsequent elements.

At the core of RNNs lies the concept of recurrent connections, which enable the network to maintain a hidden state that evolves as new elements in the sequence are processed. This hidden state captures the network's memory of previous elements, effectively introducing the element of time into neural networks. RNNs process input data one element at a time while updating the hidden state using a set of learnable parameters. The hidden state, in turn, influences the network's output and forms the basis for modeling temporal dependencies.

While RNNs hold promise for sequential data, they face challenges, notably the vanishing gradient problem. During training, gradients that flow backward through the network can diminish exponentially as they traverse multiple time steps. This phenomenon hinders learning long-range dependencies, limiting the network's ability to capture information from distant past elements in the sequence. As a result, traditional RNNs struggle to handle sequences with significant temporal gaps.

Long Short-Term Memory (or LSTM) networks and Gated Recurrent Units (or GRUs) are advanced RNN architectures designed to alleviate the vanishing gradient problem. LSTMs introduce memory cells and various gating mechanisms that enable the network to decide when to update, forget, or read information from the memory cells. GRUs simplify the LSTM architecture by merging the cell and hidden states, resulting in a more computationally efficient model. Both LSTM and GRU architectures enable RNNs to capture long-range dependencies and better understand sequences with temporal gaps.

Training RNNs involves the process of backpropagation through time (BPTT), an extension of the standard backpropagation algorithm used in feedforward neural networks. BPTT computes gradients by unrolling the network through time and applying the chain rule to calculate gradients for each time step. These gradients guide adjusting the network's parameters to reduce the distinction between the predicted and actual outcomes. While BPTT is effective, it can suffer from the vanishing gradient problem over long sequences.

The applications of RNNs span diverse domains, driven by their ability to model temporal dependencies in sequences. In natural language processing, RNNs excel in tasks like language modeling, predicting the likelihood of the next word in a sentence based on previous words. RNNs are also at the heart of machine translation, enabling systems like Google Translate to convert text from one language to another while preserving context. Time series analysis leverages RNNs to forecast stock prices, weather conditions, and other sequential data.

Bidirectional RNNs extend the capabilities of traditional RNNs by processing sequences in both forward and backward directions. This approach enables the network to capture contextual information from past and future elements, enhancing its ability to understand and predict sequences. Beyond bidirectional architectures, attention mechanisms have gained prominence, allowing RNNs to focus on specific elements in the sequence based on their relevance to the task at hand.

RNNs are not immune to challenges. They can struggle with noisy or ambiguous sequences, where inconsistent patterns may disrupt the network's memory. Additionally, training RNNs on long sequences requires substantial computational resources and can be time-consuming. Exploring techniques to mitigate noise and enhance scalability is an ongoing area of research.

Recurrent Neural Networks (RNNs) have ushered in a new era of temporal modeling, enabling machines to understand, predict, and generate sequences with remarkable accuracy. By incorporating memory mechanisms and introducing the element of time into neural networks, RNNs have unlocked the potential to unravel the intricate patterns embedded in sequences. From language modeling to time series analysis, RNNs have left an indelible mark on various domains, offering previously out of reach insights, predictions, and context. As RNNs continue, researchers and practitioners alike are poised to pioneer deeper levels of temporal understanding, ushering in a future where machines comprehend and predict sequences as naturally as human intuition.

Chapter IX

Natural Language Processing (NLP) and Text Analytics

Introduction to NLP and its Applications

Natural Language Processing (NLP) stands at the crossroads of artificial intelligence and human language, aiming to enable machines to understand, interpret, and generate human language. As humans communicate through text and speech, NLP seeks to bridge the gap between these modes of communication and computational systems. This section provides an in-depth introduction to NLP, explores its fundamental concepts, delves into its applications across diverse domains, and highlights its transformative role in reshaping human-computer interaction.

Human language is intricate, nuanced, and context-dependent, making it a formidable challenge for machines to comprehend. Words can have multiple meanings, and context often influences their interpretation. Additionally, languages exhibit variations in syntax, grammar, and cultural nuances. NLP endeavors to equip machines with the ability to navigate this complexity, enabling them to understand the semantics, sentiments, and intentions embedded within text and speech.

At the heart of NLP lie foundational techniques that transform raw text into structured data for computational analysis. Tokenization breaks text into individual words or tokens, enabling machines to process and analyze language. Part-of-Speech (POS) tagging assigns grammatical categories to words, aiding in syntactic analysis. Parsing involves analyzing the grammatical structure of sentences to extract meaning and relationships between words. These techniques provide the building blocks for more advanced NLP tasks.

Named Entity Recognition (NER) is a crucial NLP task that involves identifying and categorizing entities such as names of people, organizations, locations, and dates within text. NER finds applications in information extraction, search engines, and knowledge graph creation. On the other hand, sentiment analysis gauges the emotional tone of text, determining whether the sentiment expressed is positive, negative, or neutral. Businesses leverage sentiment analysis to gauge customer feedback, monitor brand perception, and make data-driven decisions.

Machine translation is a hallmark application of NLP, facilitating text conversion from one language to another. Technologies like Google Translate rely on NLP techniques to process and comprehend the structure of different languages, enabling seamless cross-lingual communication. Language generation takes NLP a step further by allowing machines to produce coherent and contextually relevant text. Chatbots, virtual assistants, and automated content generation are examples of systems that employ language generation to interact with users and provide information.

Question-answering systems use NLP to understand questions posed in natural language and retrieve relevant information from large datasets or knowledge bases. These systems find applications in customer support, education, and research. Information retrieval leverages NLP to help users find relevant documents, articles, or web pages based on their queries. Search engines like Google utilize NLP techniques to rank and present search results that match user intent.

NLP's transformative impact extends across industries. In healthcare, NLP aids in medical record analysis, clinical decision support, and disease diagnosis. Financial institutions use NLP for sentiment analysis of market news, customer interactions, and fraud detection. Legal professionals employ NLP for contract analysis, legal research, and document summarization. NLP is also applied in social media monitoring, content recommendation, and accessibility features such as speech recognition and text-to-speech conversion.

NLP faces inherent challenges due to the nuanced nature of human language. Ambiguity arises when a single word or phrase has multiple meanings, requiring context to disambiguate. Contextual understanding is particularly challenging, as words' meanings can change based on their surrounding text. Multilingualism introduces complexities in translating idiomatic expressions and cultural nuances accurately. Additionally, bias in training data can lead to biased language models, raising ethical concerns.

Recent advancements in NLP have been driven by deep learning, particularly the rise of transformer architectures. Transformers, exemplified by models like BERT (or Bidirectional Encoder Representations from Transformers) and GPT (or Generative Pre-trained Transformer), have revolutionized NLP by capturing contextual information and relationships between words more effectively. These models perform state-of-the-art tasks like language understanding, sentiment analysis, and machine translation.

Natural Language Processing (NLP) is a dynamic field that bridges the gap between machines and human language, transforming how we interact with computers and analyze textual data. From sentiment analysis and machine translation to question-answering and language generation, NLP applications span a spectrum of industries, enhancing communication, decision-making, and accessibility. As NLP continues to evolve, fueled by advancements in deep learning and transformers, it holds the promise of unlocking new dimensions of human-computer interaction, facilitating cross-cultural communication, and unraveling the intricate tapestry of human language for the betterment of society.

Text Preprocessing and Feature Extraction

In Natural Language Processing (NLP), the journey from raw text to meaningful insights involves intricate text preprocessing and feature extraction steps. Text data, characterized by its complexity and variability, requires careful preparation before it can be fed into NLP models. This section delves into the pivotal roles of text preprocessing and feature extraction, exploring their significance, techniques, and impact on the effectiveness of NLP applications.

Raw text, in its unprocessed form, poses challenges for NLP models. It contains punctuation, capitalization, and irregularities that hinder the algorithms' ability to extract meaningful patterns. Moreover, words can have various forms—plural, verb tenses, and conjugations—making it essential to normalize text to a standardized representation.

Text preprocessing is a transformative process that involves a series of operations to clean, normalize, and prepare the text data for analysis. Tokenization divides text into individual words or tokens, separating them from punctuation. Lowercasing ensures uniformity by converting all words to lowercase, eliminating variations due to capitalization. Stopword removal eliminates common words that add little value to analysis, such as "the," "and," and "is." Stemming and lemmatization reduce words to their root forms, addressing variations due to tense and conjugation.

Normalization techniques in text preprocessing aim to reduce variations and standardize text representations. Stemming reduces words to their base or root form by removing suffixes and prefixes. For instance, "running" and "ran" would both be reduced to "run." Lemmatization, a more advanced technique, considers the linguistic context to reduce words to their dictionary form. For example, "better" and "best" would both be lemmatized to "good."

Like articles and conjunctions, stopwords frequently appear in text but contribute minimal information. Removing stopwords can significantly reduce the dimensionality of the data and improve model efficiency. However, caution is required, as some stopwords might carry contextual significance in specific applications. For example, in sentiment analysis, the sentiment of a sentence could change drastically by removing negation words like "not."

Text data, composed of words and sentences, cannot be directly fed into most machine learning algorithms. Feature extraction transforms text data into numerical representations that algorithms can use for analysis. The bag-of-words model is a fundamental approach that represents text as a collection of words, disregarding word order. Every document is represented by a vector, with each dimension denoting a distinct word and the value denoting the frequency of that term.

Enhancing the bag-of-words model is a feature extraction technique called Term Frequency-Inverse Document Frequency (TF-IDF). It considers word frequency and balances the importance of words in a document relative to their occurrence across the entire corpus. Words that are common in a specific document but rare in the whole corpus receive a higher TF-IDF score, signifying their uniqueness and significance to that document.

Word embeddings are advanced feature extraction techniques that capture semantic relationships between words. Instead of representing words as discrete symbols, word embeddings map words to continuous vector spaces. Popular word embedding models like Word2Vec and GloVe capture semantic similarity, enabling algorithms to understand the context and relationships between words. These embeddings are pre-trained on large text corpora and can be fine-tuned for specific tasks.

The quality of text preprocessing and feature extraction significantly impacts the performance of NLP applications. In sentiment analysis, well-preprocessed data ensures that the model captures sentiment accurately. In text classification, effective feature extraction techniques enable identifying relevant features that distinguish between classes. Indexing and ranking documents based on processed text enhance search accuracy in information retrieval.

Text preprocessing is not a one-size-fits-all approach. Different domains, languages, and tasks require tailored preprocessing techniques. For example, social media text might have unconventional grammar and frequent emoticons, demanding specialized handling. Additionally, excessive preprocessing can lead to loss of context or semantic information, diminishing the quality of extracted features.

Text preprocessing and feature extraction serve as the cornerstone of successful NLP endeavors. By cleaning and standardizing text data and transforming it into numerical representations, these processes enable algorithms to uncover hidden insights and patterns. The choice of techniques depends on the data's nature and the analysis's goals. As the field of NLP continues to evolve, the art and science of data transformation through preprocessing and feature extraction remain essential skills, unlocking the true potential of NLP and revolutionizing how we understand and interact with textual information.

Sentiment Analysis and Named Entity Recognition

In Natural Language Processing (NLP), two critical tasks are cornerstones of understanding and extracting insights from text data: Sentiment Analysis and Named Entity Recognition (NER). These tasks empower machines to grasp the emotions conveyed by text and identify important entities within it. This section delves into the intricacies of Sentiment Analysis and NER, exploring their significance, methodologies, applications, and their transformative role in unraveling the layers of meaning hidden within textual content.

Sentiment Analysis, often called opinion mining, is a profound NLP task that seeks to gauge text's emotional tone or sentiment. Whether a piece of text carries a positive, negative, or neutral sentiment is paramount in understanding human communication. Sentiment Analysis has applications ranging from market research and brand monitoring to social media and customer feedback analysis.

Sentiment Analysis approaches can be broadly classified into two categories: lexicon-based and machine learning-based. Lexicon-based methods rely on sentiment dictionaries containing words and their associated sentiment scores. The frequency and intensity of words that are positive or negative in a text are used to calculate its sentiment. Machine learning-based methods, on the other hand, involve training models on labeled datasets to learn the relationships between words and sentiments. These models, such as Support Vector Machines, Naïve Bayes, and deep learning architectures, can capture complex linguistic patterns and contextual nuances.

Sentiment Analysis faces challenges rooted in the nuances of human language. Words can have different meanings in different contexts, leading to misinterpretations. Sarcasm and irony, where words convey sentiments opposite to their literal meanings, pose difficulties for sentiment analysis models. Additionally, emotions can be subtle and context-dependent, requiring a deeper understanding of the surrounding text to determine sentiment accurately.

Named Entity Recognition (NER) is a foundational NLP task that identifies and classifies named entities within text. Named entities are real-world objects such as names of people, organizations, locations, dates, and more. NER plays a pivotal role in information extraction, document summarization, search engines, and question-answering systems by enabling the identification of entities relevant to a particular context.

NER approaches encompass rule-based and machine learning-based methods. Rule-based methods rely on predefined patterns and linguistic rules to identify entities. These methods are effective for recognizing straightforward entities but may struggle with variations in names and entities with no clear patterns. Machine learning-based methods involve training models on annotated datasets to learn patterns and features that distinguish entities from non-entities. Models like Conditional Random Fields (CRF) and Bidirectional LSTM-CRF are popular choices for NER.

NER finds applications in diverse domains. In news analysis, NER helps identify the names of people, organizations, and locations mentioned in articles. In biomedical literature, NER assists in extracting gene names, protein names, and disease names. In legal documents, NER can identify contract parties and key terms. By identifying entities, NER enhances information extraction, enabling automated systems to summarize, categorize, and retrieve relevant content.

NER grapples with challenges related to entity ambiguity and multilingualism. Ambiguity arises when entities share names with common words. For instance, "Apple" could refer to the fruit or the technology company. Multilingual NER is complex due to variations in language structures and entity names across different languages. Transliteration, the process of representing names in a different script, adds another layer of difficulty.

Sentiment Analysis and NER are not isolated tasks; they often complement each other in text analysis. NER provides contextual information that can enhance sentiment analysis by identifying named entities. For instance, understanding the sentiment of comments about a product or service becomes more insightful when paired with identifying the entities involved, such as the product name and company. Conversely, sentiment analysis can enrich NER by providing emotional context to the entities identified.

Sentiment Analysis and Named Entity Recognition are integral threads in the intricate tapestry of NLP, enabling machines to decode the myriad layers of meaning within textual content. Sentiment Analysis uncovers the emotional context of text, offering insights into human sentiments and opinions. Named Entity Recognition identifies and classifies significant entities, enriching information extraction and context understanding. Together, these tasks empower NLP systems to comprehend, categorize, and extract insights from text, bridging the gap between human language's intricacies and machines' analytical power. As NLP continues to evolve, the synergy between Sentiment Analysis and NER promises to unlock new dimensions of understanding, enabling us to unravel the stories hidden within text and harness the potential of textual data in unprecedented ways.

Chapter X

Big Data Technologies
and Frameworks

Apache Hadoop and Hadoop Ecosystem

In the landscape of Big Data, Apache Hadoop has emerged as a game-changing framework that revolutionizes how large volumes of data are processed, stored, and analyzed. Hadoop's distributed design and extensive tool ecosystem are becoming essential for enterprises looking to extract insights and value from their data assets as the volume and complexity of data keeps on increasing. This section delves into the foundations of Apache Hadoop, explores its core components, and highlights its diverse ecosystem, shaping the landscape of modern data processing and analytics.

The birth of Apache Hadoop can be traced back to the early 2000s when Doug Cutting and Mike Cafarella created it as an open-source project to tackle the challenges posed by ever-increasing volumes of data. Hadoop's design was inspired by Google's MapReduce framework, enabling it to distribute and parallelize data processing across clusters of commodity hardware. Hadoop's decentralized approach to data storage and processing was a paradigm shift, allowing organizations to harness the power of distributed computing to analyze massive datasets efficiently.

At the heart of Hadoop lies the Hadoop Distributed File System (HDFS), which is responsible for storing as well as managing vast amounts of data across a cluster of machines. HDFS divides data into blocks and replicates them across different nodes to ensure fault tolerance. Data locality is a key principle in HDFS, enabling computational tasks to be executed closer to where the data resides.

MapReduce is the programming model and processing engine that drives Hadoop's data processing capabilities. It divides tasks into smaller subtasks and processes them in parallel across the cluster. Map tasks process and transform data, while Reduce tasks aggregate and analyze the results. This divide-and-conquer approach facilitates scalable processing of large datasets, making it possible to tackle complex analyses that were previously unfeasible.

The Hadoop ecosystem is a constellation of tools and frameworks built around the core Hadoop components, catering to various aspects of data processing, storage, and analytics. Apache Hive, for instance, provides a SQL-like query language that allows users to query and analyze data stored in HDFS, making Big Data analytics more accessible to analysts and business users. Apache Pig offers a high-level scripting language for data processing, abstracting the complexities of MapReduce programming.

Apache HBase is a NoSQL database that operates on top of HDFS, designed for fast random read and write access to large datasets.

HBase is particularly suited for applications that require real-time data access, such as sensor data analysis and social media monitoring. Apache Spark, another prominent ecosystem component, introduces in-memory processing and a more flexible programming model than MapReduce. It supports batch processing, interactive querying, machine learning, and graph processing.

The introduction of YARN (or Yet Another Resource Negotiator) marked a significant evolution in Hadoop's architecture. YARN decouples resource management from data processing, allowing multiple processing frameworks to share resources efficiently. This decoupling enables Hadoop clusters to support a broader range of workloads beyond MapReduce, such as Spark, Flink, and more. YARN enhances cluster utilization, enabling the running of various applications concurrently and optimizing resource allocation.

While Hadoop has transformed the field of Big Data, it's not without challenges. The framework was initially designed for batch processing, making real-time data analysis a limitation. As organizations sought to analyze data as it arrives, new tools and frameworks like Apache Kafka and Apache Flink emerged to address this gap. These advancements facilitate real-time stream processing, enabling organizations to extract insights from streaming data sources such as IoT devices and social media feeds.

Apache Hadoop and its ecosystem are pillars of the data-driven future, democratizing access to Big Data processing and analytics. Hadoop's distributed architecture, coupled with its rich array of tools, empowers organizations to process, store, and gain insights from massive datasets that were previously unimaginable. From HDFS to MapReduce, YARN to Spark, the Hadoop ecosystem provides a versatile toolkit that adapts to evolving data challenges. As the digital universe continues to expand, Apache Hadoop's enduring legacy lies in its ability to lay the foundation for data-driven decision-making, innovation, and transformation across industries, propelling us toward a future where data is not just a challenge, but a boundless opportunity.

Apache Spark for In-Memory Data Processing

In the realm of Big Data analytics, the need for quickly and efficiently processing large volumes of data has driven the evolution of frameworks that can keep pace with the demands of modern data processing. Among these, Apache Spark has emerged as a transformative force, offering in-memory data processing capabilities that enable organizations to perform complex analyses at unprecedented speeds. This section explores the foundations of Apache Spark, delves into its architecture and core concepts, and highlights its significance in data processing and analytics.

Apache Spark's journey began in the UC Berkeley AMPLab in 2009, where researchers recognized the limitations of existing Big Data processing frameworks. While Hadoop's MapReduce brought scalability to the forefront, it suffered from disk-based processing, which led to slow execution times for iterative algorithms and machine learning tasks. Apache Spark was designed to address this limitation by leveraging in-memory computing, accelerating data processing and analytics by several orders of magnitude.

At the core of Spark's in-memory processing lies the Resilient Distributed Datasets (RDDs) concept. RDDs are fault-tolerant, immutable data structures that allow users to perform distributed computations on data residing in memory. By maintaining lineage information, RDDs ensure fault tolerance by enabling data to be re-computed in the event of a node failure. This fault-tolerance mechanism and the ability to cache data in memory form the basis for Spark's in-memory data processing paradigm.

Spark's architecture centers around a master-slave model, where a driver program coordinates tasks across worker nodes. RDDs, as the primary abstraction, enable Spark to handle various types of workloads, including batch processing, interactive querying, machine learning, and graph processing. Spark's flexibility stems from its ability to seamlessly transition between different data processing modes while leveraging in-memory capabilities for enhanced performance.

Spark's programming model is characterized by two types of operations: transformations and actions. Transformations are operations that generate new RDDs from existing ones, such as map, filter, and join. These operations exhibit laziness, meaning they are not executed immediately but create a lineage of transformations to be applied later. Conversely, actions trigger the actual computation and return results to the driver program, allowing users to retrieve insights from their data.

Apache Spark's in-memory data processing capabilities have revolutionized analytics in various domains. Traditional data processing frameworks often necessitated time-consuming disk I/O operations, limiting the speed at which analyses could be performed. Spark's ability to keep data in memory and process it in parallel across nodes has unlocked new realms of possibility, enabling real-time analytics, iterative algorithms, and machine learning tasks that were previously infeasible.

Spark's ecosystem has expanded beyond its core functionalities to encompass many libraries and tools. Apache Spark SQL brings structured data processing to the Spark framework, allowing users to query and manipulate data using SQL-like syntax. Libraries like MLlib offer machine learning capabilities, enabling users to build as well as train machine learning models at scale. Spark Streaming extends Spark's capabilities to real-time data processing, while GraphX provides graph processing and analysis tools.

Advancements beyond in-memory processing have marked Apache Spark's journey. Introducing Catalyst, Spark's query optimizer, has enhanced query performance and optimization. Furthermore, Spark's compatibility with popular programming languages like Scala, Python, and Java has contributed to its widespread adoption. However, challenges persist in handling massive datasets that may exceed memory capacity and optimizing Spark's performance for specific workloads.

Apache Spark's emergence as a powerhouse in Big Data processing is a testament to the need for speed, scalability, and efficiency in modern data analytics. By harnessing the power of in-memory computing and offering a versatile ecosystem of tools and libraries,

Spark has transformed the data processing landscape, enabling organizations to unlock insights from massive datasets in real-time. As the digital universe continues to expand, Apache Spark stands as a beacon of innovation, sparking a revolution in data processing that paves the way for a future where the limits of data analytics are bound only by our imagination.

Other Big Data Tools: Cassandra, HBase, etc.

In the era of Big Data, the diversity and complexity of data sources have given rise to many tools and technologies to tackle the challenges of data storage, management, and analysis. While Apache Hadoop and Spark dominate the landscape, various other tools have emerged to address specific requirements and use cases. This section delves into some of these tools, including Apache Cassandra, Apache HBase, and more, highlighting their significance, core features, and applications in the world of Big Data.

Apache Cassandra, a distributed NoSQL database, is a key player in the world of Big Data. In order to manage massive volumes of data across numerous nodes and data centers, scalability, availability, and fault tolerance are given top priority in Cassandra. Its decentralized architecture and peer-to-peer design eliminate single points of failure, making it suitable for applications demanding high availability and low-latency performance.

Cassandra's data model revolves around column families, allowing for flexible schema design. Its write-optimized architecture excels at handling write-heavy workloads, making it a popular choice for use cases such as time-series data, sensor data, and logging. Cassandra's support for tunable consistency levels and eventual consistency empowers users to tailor data consistency to their application's requirements.

Apache HBase, another significant player, is an open-source, distributed, column-oriented database that provides real-time read and write access to large datasets. Built on top of Hadoop's HDFS, HBase brings the power of distributed storage to NoSQL databases. HBase's architecture is reminiscent of Google's Bigtable, offering high scalability and performance for applications demanding random read and write access patterns.

HBase stores data in a sparse, multidimensional map structure, where a unique row key identifies rows, and each row can have multiple columns. This design is particularly well-suited for use cases involving time-series data, social media data, and real-time analytics. HBase's ability to handle rapid insertions and updates of data while maintaining high throughput has made it a favorite for applications that require low-latency data access.

Beyond Cassandra and HBase, other NoSQL databases have gained prominence in the Big Data landscape. MongoDB, a document-oriented database, stores data in flexible JSON-like documents, offering schema flexibility and horizontal scalability. MongoDB's query language and indexing capabilities make it well-suited for applications requiring rich semi-structured data queries.

Couchbase, a distributed NoSQL database, combines the flexibility of document databases with the performance and scalability of key-value stores. Couchbase's architecture includes a caching layer that enhances data retrieval speeds. It finds applications in use cases requiring low-latency data access, such as online gaming and real-time recommendation engines.

Elasticsearch, a distributed search and analytics engine, focuses on full-text search capabilities and real-time data analysis. Large volumes of textual data may be indexed and queried with great power and scalability due to Elasticsearch, which is constructed on top of the Lucene search library. It supports complex queries, aggregations, and geospatial search, making it suitable for log analysis, content discovery, and monitoring applications.

Elasticsearch's popularity has grown due to its ease of use, RESTful API, and rich ecosystem of plugins. It integrates well with other tools and can be combined with Kibana and Logstash to create the famous ELK (Elasticsearch, Logstash, Kibana) stack for log analysis and visualization.

The Big Data landscape is a dynamic ecosystem filled with diverse tools, each designed to address specific challenges and use cases. Apache Cassandra and HBase excel in distributed, high-throughput storage scenarios, while MongoDB and Couchbase cater to applications requiring flexibility in schema design. Elasticsearch empowers real-time search and analysis, unlocking insights from textual data. These tools, alongside Hadoop and Spark, form a comprehensive toolbox that organizations can wield to extract value from the vast sea of data. As the Big Data field continues to evolve, these tools play an integral role in shaping the data-driven future, offering solutions that align with organizations' specific needs and aspirations across industries.

Chapter XI

Data Ethics and Privacy

Ethical Considerations in Data Collection and Use

Data has emerged as a valuable resource in the digital age, fueling advancements in technology, science, and business. However, data collection's increasing volume and depth raise critical ethical questions about privacy, consent, bias, and accountability. As organizations and individuals harness data for insights and decision-making, the need for responsible and ethical data practices becomes paramount. This section delves into the ethical considerations surrounding data collection and use, exploring the implications, challenges, and guidelines that shape our evolving digital landscape.

The proliferation of data collection technologies has heightened concerns about individual privacy. Individuals' digital footprints through online interactions, social media, and connected devices paint a detailed portrait of their lives. The ethical dilemma lies in striking a balance between extracting valuable insights from this data and respecting individuals' privacy rights. Organizations must consider the principles of data minimization, purpose limitation, and informed consent to ensure that data collection aligns with user expectations and legal frameworks.

Obtaining knowledgeable consent is a cornerstone of ethical data practices. Individuals should clearly understand how their data will be used, by whom, and for what purposes. Informed consent empowers individuals to make informed decisions about sharing their data, allowing them to weigh the benefits against the risks. However, challenges arise in obtaining meaningful consent in complex digital ecosystems where terms of use are often buried in lengthy agreements. Maintaining transparency and simplicity in consent processes is vital to upholding ethical standards.

The data used for analysis often carries inherent biases that can result in unfair or discriminatory outcomes. Biased data can perpetuate social, racial, and gender inequalities if not correctly addressed. Ethical data analysis requires a commitment to recognizing and rectifying biases through techniques like data preprocessing, bias-aware algorithms, and diversity-aware training. Acknowledging data sources' limitations and potential biases is essential to guarantee that the insights derived are accurate, fair, and representative.

With great data power comes great ethical responsibility. Organizations must take ownership of their data collection and usage practices. They should follow data protection laws, put safety measures in place to protect sensitive data, and create clear standards for managing data. As the data custodians, organizations must be prepared to answer questions about the ethics of their data practices, fostering a culture of accountability that extends from the boardroom to the development teams.

The monetization of data introduces a complex ethical landscape. Organizations often collect data for profit, leading to questions about the value exchange between data subjects and data collectors. Ethical considerations involve ensuring that individuals receive fair compensation or benefits for their data contributions, especially in cases where third parties monetize data. Data monetization models should align with transparency, accountability, and the principles of fair compensation.

Addressing ethical concerns in data collection and use requires the adoption of ethical guidelines and frameworks. Initiatives like the Fair Information Practice Principles (FIPPs) and the General Data Protection Regulation (GDPR) set data protection, consent, and accountability standards. Developing ethical AI and data ethics committees within organizations underscores the commitment to responsible data practices. Embracing these guidelines ensures data is harnessed ethically, respecting individuals' rights and societal values.

In an era where data underpins progress and innovation, ethical considerations are the compass that guides our digital journey. Responsible data collection and usage practices are not just legal obligations but ethical imperatives safeguarding individual rights, societal values, and the integrity of data-driven decision-making. As organizations and individuals navigate the complexities of data collection, they must strive for transparency, informed consent, fairness, and accountability. Embracing a culture of ethical data stewardship ensures that the transformative power of data is harnessed for the betterment of society while respecting the fundamental principles that define our digital age.

Ensuring Data Privacy and Security

In the digital transformation era, where data is the lifeblood of modern enterprises and individuals, ensuring data privacy and security has become a paramount concern. The exponential growth of data and the increasing sophistication of cyber threats have highlighted the urgency of safeguarding sensitive information. As organizations and individuals navigate the digital landscape, the need to protect data from unauthorized access, breaches, and misuse has never been more critical. This section explores the dimensions of data privacy and security, delving into the challenges, best practices, and technological solutions underpinning the digital frontier's fortification.

Data breaches, identity theft, and cyberattacks have demonstrated the severe consequences of inadequate data privacy and security measures. Personal, financial, and proprietary information can be exploited, leading to financial losses, reputational damage, and violation of individual rights. The interconnected nature of the digital world amplifies the ripple effects of data breaches, underscoring the necessity of proactive measures to safeguard data integrity, confidentiality, and availability.

The evolving threat landscape presents multifaceted challenges to data privacy and security. Cybercriminals employ diverse attack vectors to infiltrate systems and networks, including phishing, ransomware, and social engineering. Insider threats, arising from employees with access to sensitive data, also pose risks. Moreover, the global nature of data transfer and storage complicates regulatory compliance, as data protection laws vary across jurisdictions. Striking a balance between convenience and security further challenges organizations and individuals in their data privacy journey.

Encryption stands as one of the fundamental pillars of data privacy and security. Encryption assures that even if unwanted parties gain access to data, they cannot decipher what it contains without the associated decryption key by changing it into an unreadable format using cryptographic techniques. End-to-end encryption protects data during transmission and storage, preventing eavesdropping and unauthorized access. Advances in encryption techniques, such as homomorphic encryption, enable computations on encrypted data, preserving privacy while allowing for meaningful analysis.

Access controls and authentication mechanisms play a pivotal role in data security. Implementing role-based access controls (RBAC) ensures that only authorized users can access specific data and perform certain actions. Multi-factor authentication (MFA), requiring multiple forms of identity verification, adds an extra layer of security. Strong password policies and biometric authentication techniques, like fingerprint and facial recognition, bolster access controls and safeguard data from unauthorized access.

Adopting data minimization practices involves collecting and retaining only the necessary data to fulfill a specific purpose. By reducing the volume of stored data, organizations limit the potential impact of a breach. Implementing data retention policies ensures that data is retained for the required duration and securely disposed of afterward. Data anonymization and pseudonymization techniques add an extra layer of protection by de-identifying sensitive information.

Data privacy regulations, such General Data Protection Regulation and California Consumer Privacy Act (CCPA), impose legal obligations on organizations to protect individuals' data and provide transparency in data practices. Compliance with these regulations involves clear communication of data usage, obtaining consent, and allowing individuals to exercise their rights regarding their data. Failure to comply can lead to massive fines and reputational damage, making regulatory adherence a crucial aspect of data privacy and security.

Artificial Intelligence and also machine learning are driving data privacy and security innovations. AI-powered algorithms can analyze vast datasets to detect real-time anomalies and potential security breaches. Privacy-preserving techniques, such as federated learning and differential privacy, allow organizations to gain insights from data without compromising individual privacy. These technologies enable collaboration and data analysis while maintaining data confidentiality.

Amidst technological advancements, the human element remains critical in ensuring data privacy and security. Cybersecurity education and training programs empower individuals to recognize phishing attempts, understand security best practices, and adopt responsible digital behaviors. A culture of security awareness within organizations and society at large is pivotal in thwarting cyber threats and minimizing the risk of data breaches.

In the digital age, where data fuels innovation and progress, the responsibility to ensure data privacy and security is a shared endeavor. Organizations, individuals, and governments must collaboratively work to implement robust security measures, adhere to data protection regulations, and stay informed about emerging threats. Encryption, access controls, and regulatory compliance are tools to safeguard data integrity and confidentiality. The convergence of technology and human vigilance creates a resilient defense against cyber threats, enabling us to confidently embrace the digital future while preserving the sanctity of our data and the trust of those we serve.

Regulatory Compliance (e.g., GDPR) and Best Practices

In the digital age, the proliferation of data and technology has led to a heightened concern for data privacy and security. Governments and regulatory bodies worldwide have responded by introducing data protection regulations to safeguard individuals' rights and hold organizations accountable for responsible data handling. One of the most prominent and far-reaching regulations is the General Data Protection Regulation, abbreviated as GDPR implemented by the European Union (EU). This section delves into the intricacies of regulatory compliance, focusing on GDPR, and explores best practices that organizations can adopt to ensure they navigate the data privacy landscape ethically and effectively.

The GDPR, enacted by the EU in 2018, stands as a landmark legislation in data protection. Designed to balance data privacy laws across EU member states and grant individuals greater control over their personal data, GDPR has far-reaching implications for organizations both within and outside the EU. Its core principles include transparency, consent, purpose limitation, data minimization, accuracy, storage limitation, integrity, and accountability. Organizations that process personal data of EU citizens must comply with these principles or face significant fines and reputational damage.

GDPR's multifaceted framework addresses a wide range of data privacy aspects. It mandates that organizations obtain clear and informed consent before collecting personal data, and individuals can withdraw consent at any time. GDPR enforces the right to access, rectify, and erase personal data, also known as the "right to be forgotten." Data subjects have the right to data portability, allowing them to move their data from one service provider to another. Organizations must also report data breaches to the relevant authorities and affected individuals within a specified timeframe.

Under GDPR, organizations that process large amounts of personal data or engage in systematic monitoring must appoint a Data Protection Officer (DPO). The DPO bridges the organization and data protection authorities, ensuring that data processing activities adhere to GDPR's provisions. Accountability is a central tenet of GDPR, compelling organizations to demonstrate compliance with the regulation. This involves maintaining records of processing activities, conducting data protection impact assessments, and implementing measures to ensure the ongoing security and confidentiality of data.

Organizations can adopt a range of best practices to navigate the intricate terrain of regulatory compliance. The first step involves understanding the scope of data processing activities and identifying the types of personal data being collected and processed. Implementing a comprehensive data protection policy that outlines the organization's commitment to GDPR compliance is crucial. Organizations should also establish mechanisms for obtaining valid and explicit consent from data subjects, ensuring that permission is freely given, informed, and specific to the intended purposes.

Implementing robust data security measures, including encryption, access controls, and regular security audits, is essential to safeguard personal data from breaches. Organizations should also appoint a Data Protection Officer (DPO) if required, and ensure that employees receive proper training on data protection policies and practices. Transparent communication with data subjects about data processing activities, their rights, and how they can exercise those rights fosters trust and demonstrates the organization's commitment to data privacy.

GDPR places restrictions on the transfer of personal data to countries outside the EU that do not offer an adequate level of data protection. Organizations engaging in international data transfers must employ safeguards including Standard Contractual Clauses (or

SCCs) or Binding Corporate Rules (or BCRs) to protect personal data. Additionally, when engaging third-party processors to handle personal data, organizations must establish clear data processing agreements that outline the responsibilities of both parties in complying with GDPR.

Regulatory compliance is not a one-time effort but an ongoing commitment. Organizations must continuously monitor and assess their data processing activities to ensure compliance with GDPR principles. Regular audits and reviews of data protection policies and practices help identify areas for improvement and address emerging risks. GDPR compliance requires organizations to adapt to evolving data privacy landscapes, technological advancements, and changes in data processing activities.

In an era where data-driven innovation is transforming industries, ethical data guardianship has emerged as a moral and legal imperative. The General Data Protection Regulation (GDPR) encapsulates the principles of data protection, consent, transparency, and accountability. As organizations operate in an increasingly interconnected world, adhering to GDPR and adopting best practices in data protection not only safeguards individual rights but also fosters trust, enhances organizational reputation, and strengthens the data ecosystem as a whole. By placing data privacy at the heart of their operations, organizations contribute to a digital landscape characterized by respect for individuals' autonomy and protecting their most valuable asset: personal data.

Chapter XII

Real-world Applications
of Data Science and Big Data Analytics

Healthcare and Medical Data Analysis

In the modern era, the convergence of healthcare and data analysis has ignited a transformational journey that promises to improve patient outcomes, enhance medical research, and revolutionize the healthcare industry. The sheer volume of medical data generated through electronic health records (EHRs), medical imaging, wearable devices, and genomics has paved the way for data-driven insights that were once unimaginable. This section delves into the realm of healthcare and medical data analysis, exploring the challenges, opportunities, and profound impact that data analytics is having on the delivery of healthcare services and the advancement of medical science.

Abundant data, from patient medical histories to clinical trial results, have long characterized the healthcare industry. However, the transition from paper-based records to digital platforms has exponentially increased the availability and accessibility of medical data. Electronic Health Records (EHRs) store comprehensive patient information, enabling clinicians to make informed decisions, track patient progress, and coordinate care more effectively. Medical imaging, such as MRI and CT scans, generates vast amounts of visual data that can be analyzed to diagnose diseases and assess treatment efficacy.

Medical data analysis lays the foundation for personalized medicine, an approach that tailors healthcare interventions to the individual characteristics of each patient. Genomic data, obtained through DNA sequencing, provides insights into an individual's genetic makeup, disease susceptibility, and potential treatment responses. By analyzing genomic data alongside clinical and lifestyle information, healthcare practitioners can predict disease risk, recommend personalized treatments, and optimize preventive care strategies. Personalized medicine improves patient outcomes, minimizes adverse effects, and reduces healthcare costs.

Integrating data analytics into healthcare systems has paved the way for predictive modeling and early disease detection. By leveraging historical patient data, machine learning algorithms can determine patterns and trends that may indicate the onset of certain medical conditions. Predictive analytics can flag patients at risk of developing chronic diseases, allowing for timely interventions and preventive measures. In critical care, real-time patient data monitoring can alert medical staff to deteriorating conditions, enabling rapid responses and improved patient outcomes.

Medical data analysis is revolutionizing medical research and drug discovery. Analyzing large datasets of patient information can reveal novel insights into disease mechanisms, treatment responses, and genetic factors. In drug discovery, data-driven approaches accelerate the identification of potential drug candidates and forecast their efficacy. Virtual clinical trials, enabled by data simulation and modeling, offer an alternative to traditional trials, reducing costs, and accelerating drug development timelines. By leveraging data analytics, researchers can make informed decisions and bring life-saving treatments to market more efficiently.

While medical data analysis holds immense potential, it also brings challenges and ethical considerations. Patient privacy and data security are paramount, particularly in an era of rising data breaches and cyber threats. Striking a balance between data utilization for research and ensuring patient confidentiality requires robust data anonymization and encryption techniques. Ethical considerations also extend to data ownership, consent, and the potential biases that may arise from analyzing diverse patient populations.

One of the challenges in medical data analysis lies in the interoperability of various data sources. EHRs, medical devices, and wearable technologies often produce data in different formats and standards. Integrating these disparate data sources is essential for a comprehensive view of patient health. The development of Health Information Exchanges (HIEs) and standardized data formats aims to address this challenge, allowing for seamless data exchange and analysis across healthcare systems.

The convergence of healthcare and data analysis marks a significant paradigm shift in the way healthcare is delivered. Data-driven care delivery emphasizes evidence-based decision-making, personalized interventions, and proactive disease management. Wearable devices and remote monitoring tools empower patients to actively participate in their healthcare journeys, while AI-powered diagnostic tools enhance clinical accuracy and efficiency. Telemedicine and virtual care models, enabled by data analysis, expand access to healthcare services and cater to the evolving needs of patients.

The marriage of healthcare and medical data analysis has unlocked a realm of possibilities that extends beyond traditional medical practices. As the healthcare industry embraces data-driven insights, patients can expect more personalized care, earlier disease detection, and improved treatment outcomes. Medical research is propelled by the vast datasets at its disposal, accelerating drug discovery and uncovering novel disease insights. While data security, privacy, and interoperability challenges persist, the ability to transform patient care and medical knowledge is undeniable. The fusion of technology, data, and healthcare expertise reshapes the healthcare landscape, creating a future where data-driven decisions are at the heart of every medical endeavor.

Business Intelligence and Market Insights

Data has emerged as a powerful ally in today's rapidly evolving business landscape, guiding organizations toward informed decision-making and competitive advantage. The fusion of data analysis and business intelligence (BI) has given rise to a new era of strategic understanding, where organizations harness insights from vast datasets to drive growth, enhance operational efficiency, and capture market opportunities. This section delves into business intelligence and market insights, exploring how data-driven strategies illuminate the path to strategic success, transform decision-making processes, and enable organizations to thrive in an increasingly dynamic marketplace.

Business intelligence is the compass that navigates organizations through complex markets and shifting customer demands. At its core, BI encompasses the processes, technologies, and tools that transform raw data into actionable insights. Organizations gain a comprehensive view of their operations, market trends, and competitive landscapes by gathering, analyzing, and visualizing data. BI empowers stakeholders at all levels to make well-informed decisions based on data-driven evidence, ultimately driving growth, innovation, and operational excellence.

In a business landscape characterized by uncertainty and competition, market insights are a strategic advantage that organizations cannot overlook. The convergence of data sources, including customer interactions, sales figures, social media sentiment, and industry trends, offers a wealth of information that can shape market strategies. Market insights unveil customer preferences, uncover emerging trends, and identify untapped opportunities. With these insights, organizations can tailor their offerings, optimize marketing campaigns, and proactively address market shifts.

Effective communication of data-driven insights is crucial to BI's success. Data visualization techniques transform complex datasets into digestible visual formats, including charts, graphs, and interactive dashboards. Visualization not only simplifies the interpretation of data but also uncovers patterns, correlations, and outliers that might otherwise go unnoticed. Interactive dashboards empower decision-makers to explore data from different angles, facilitating quicker, more informed choices.

Integrating predictive analytics within business intelligence adds a layer of foresight to decision-making. Organizations can predict future trends, customer behavior, and market shifts by leveraging historical data and advanced algorithms. Predictive analytics enable proactive strategies, such as inventory management optimization, personalized marketing recommendations, and dynamic pricing models. Organizations are able to remain ahead of the competition and take advantage of novel opportunities by using this proactive approach.

Competitive intelligence, a subset of business intelligence, focuses on gathering and analyzing information about competitors, industry trends, and market dynamics. It gives organizations a comprehensive understanding of their competitive landscape, enabling them to identify strengths, weaknesses, opportunities, and threats. Armed with competitive intelligence, organizations can refine their positioning, differentiate their offerings, and develop strategies that capitalize on market gaps.

Effective business intelligence relies on accurate, reliable, and well-managed data. Data governance frameworks ensure data is appropriately managed, protected, and compliant with regulations. Ensuring data quality involves processes to identify and rectify errors, inconsistencies, and redundancies in the data. High-quality data is the foundation for accurate insights, robust analysis, and confident decision-making.

While business intelligence offers substantial benefits, it also presents challenges and ethical considerations. The acquisition, storage, and analysis of vast amounts of data raise concerns about data privacy, security, and responsible use. Organizations must adhere to data protection regulations, gain informed consent, and anonymize sensitive information. Ethical considerations extend to data sharing and transparency, ensuring stakeholders understand how their data is used and its potential impact on their privacy.

The rapid pace of change in the business environment demands agility and adaptability in BI strategies. Organizations must be equipped to swiftly adjust their analytics models, data sources, and visualization techniques in response to market shifts. Cloud-based BI solutions enable scalability and flexibility, allowing organizations to access insights from anywhere while adapting to changing business requirements.

Business intelligence and market insights are not mere luxuries but essential ingredients in the recipe for strategic success. As organizations navigate a world of data abundance, harnessing insights from the data ecosystem is no longer optional but imperative. Data-driven decision-making, fueled by business intelligence capabilities, empowers organizations to seize opportunities, mitigate risks, and make choices grounded in evidence. Market insights illuminate the path forward, enabling organizations to survive and thrive in a dynamic business landscape. By embracing the power of business intelligence and market insights, organizations can embark on a journey that transforms data into a competitive edge, propelling them toward strategic success and a brighter future.

Social Media and Sentiment Analysis

The advent of social media has revolutionized the way individuals communicate, connect, and express themselves. It has also become a treasure trove of unfiltered opinions, emotions, and sentiments that hold immense value for businesses, organizations, and even policymakers. An effective technique for interpreting the attitudes and feelings present in online interactions, sentiment analysis was developed in response to the growing volume of social media content and the need to glean useful insights from this expansive digital environment. This section delves into social media and sentiment analysis, exploring how this dynamic duo offers organizations unprecedented opportunities to understand public sentiment, enhance customer engagement, and shape effective strategies.

Social media platforms have transformed into bustling virtual ecosystems where individuals share thoughts, opinions, and experiences on a global scale. From Instagram and LinkedIn in addition to Facebook and Twitter, billions of users engage in conversations that range from personal anecdotes to political debates. Organizations recognize the potential of this digital universe to obtain insights into customer preferences, industry trends, and public sentiment. By tapping into social media, organizations can monitor brand mentions, identify emerging trends, and engage directly with their target audience in real time.

At the heart of the social media landscape lies many emotions—joy, anger, sadness, excitement, and more—expressed through text, images, and videos. Sentiment analysis, or opinion mining, employs natural language processing and machine learning strategies to sift through this sea of digital expressions and classify them into positive, negative, or neutral sentiments. Beyond polarity, sentiment analysis can capture nuances, identifying specific emotions and even the intensity of sentiments. By deciphering the emotional context of social media content, organizations gain actionable insights that can drive strategic decision-making.

For businesses, sentiment analysis offers a direct conduit to customer sentiment. Monitoring social media conversations can reveal customers' opinions about products, services, and brand experiences. Positive sentiments can be leveraged to enhance marketing campaigns and customer testimonials, while negative sentiments can flag issues that require immediate attention. Real-time sentiment analysis enables brands to engage in timely interventions, address customer concerns, and nurture brand loyalty. By taking a proactive approach, you may improve customer satisfaction and guarantee that products and services meet customer expectations.

In the age of social media, a brand's reputation can be built or shattered in a matter of minutes. Sentiment analysis acts as a vigilant guardian, alerting organizations to shifts in public perception. By monitoring sentiment trends over time, organizations can gauge the effectiveness of their strategies, campaigns, and crisis management efforts. This continuous feedback loop enables brands to adapt swiftly, mitigate potential damage, and craft narratives that resonate positively with their audience.

Social media's real-time nature offers a unique opportunity for market insights that traditional research methods may struggle to match. Sentiment analysis enables "social listening"—the practice of monitoring and analyzing social media conversations about specific topics, trends, or products. This approach gives organizations a pulse on public sentiment, emerging trends, and competitors' strategies. The insights derived from social listening can guide product development, inform marketing strategies, and help organizations stay ahead of market shifts.

While sentiment analysis holds immense potential, it also faces challenges rooted in human language and emotion complexities. Sarcasm, irony, cultural nuances, and context can all impact sentiment classification accuracy. Developing models that understand subtleties and cultural differences requires ongoing refinement. Furthermore, sentiment analysis tools may struggle with multilingual content, dialects, and slang. Organizations must remain vigilant and employ human validation to ensure the reliability of sentiment analysis results.

As with any technology, sentiment analysis brings forth ethical considerations. Ensuring user privacy, obtaining consent, and transparently communicating data usage are essential in the era of data protection regulations. Bias can also affect sentiment analysis outcomes, as algorithms may inadvertently amplify biases present in training data. Mitigating bias and maintaining ethical data practices are crucial to prevent unintended consequences and ensure the responsible application of sentiment analysis.

Exciting advancements and applications mark the future of sentiment analysis. Emotion detection from images and videos, sentiment analysis in multilingual and code-switching contexts, and the incorporation of contextual information are areas ripe for innovation. Moreover, sentiment analysis can extend beyond marketing to domains like public policy, healthcare, and politics. Understanding public sentiment on social issues and policy decisions can inform governance and enhance citizen engagement.

Social media and sentiment analysis fusion has birthed a new dimension of data-driven decision-making. Organizations are no longer bystanders in the digital conversation but active participants, attuned to the nuances of public sentiment. By leveraging sentiment analysis, they can harness the collective emotions of individuals and translate them into strategies that resonate, engage, and drive success. From enhancing brand reputation to fine-tuning marketing campaigns, sentiment analysis is a symphony conductor, orchestrating organizations' efforts toward harmony with their audience's emotions. As social media continues to evolve, sentiment analysis emerges as a conductor's baton, guiding organizations in creating harmonious strategies that captivate hearts, minds, and markets.

Predictive Maintenance in Manufacturing

In modern manufacturing, where efficiency and productivity are paramount, the emergence of predictive maintenance has revolutionized how industries manage their equipment and assets. Predictive maintenance leverages the power of data analytics, machine learning, in addition to the Internet of Things (IoT) to foresee equipment failures, optimize maintenance schedules, and minimize downtime. This paradigm shift from reactive to proactive maintenance strategies holds the potential to enhance operational efficiency, extend equipment lifespans, and transform manufacturing processes. This section delves into the world of predictive maintenance in manufacturing, exploring its benefits, challenges, and the transformative role it plays in reshaping the industrial landscape.

Traditionally, manufacturing industries relied on reactive and preventive maintenance strategies. Reactive maintenance involves addressing equipment failures as they occur, often resulting in unexpected downtime, production halts, and costly repairs. On the other hand, preventive maintenance follows predetermined schedules for maintenance tasks, aiming to prevent failures before they occur. While these approaches have served their purpose, they are characterized by inefficiencies, over-maintenance, and the risk of unexpected downtime.

Predictive maintenance transcends these limitations by capitalizing on data analytics, machine learning algorithms, and sensor technology. It operates on the principle of leveraging real-time data from equipment sensors to monitor performance, detect anomalies, and predict potential failures. By analyzing historical data, sensor readings, and patterns of equipment behavior, predictive maintenance algorithms can forecast when a component is likely to fail. This foresight enables organizations to conduct maintenance activities precisely when needed, minimizing downtime and optimizing resource allocation.

Predictive maintenance transforms manufacturing operations by providing unprecedented insights into equipment health and performance. Real-time sensor data monitoring generates a comprehensive understanding of how machines operate under different conditions. By collecting and also analyzing this data, organizations can identify wear and tear patterns, assess the impact of varying production parameters, and uncover the root causes of equipment failures. These insights enable better maintenance planning and guide process optimization and continuous improvement initiatives.

One of the primary advantages of predictive maintenance is its potential for substantial cost savings. Organizations avoid the costly consequences of unplanned downtime, rushed repairs, and emergency parts orders by addressing maintenance needs before equipment failure occurs. Maintenance activities become more efficient, as tasks are performed when they are most needed, minimizing the need for frequent, disruptive maintenance. Moreover, predictive maintenance optimizes spare parts inventory management, making sure that the right parts are available when required.

Predictive maintenance not only enhances operational efficiency but also extends the lifespan of critical equipment. By identifying and addressing potential issues early, organizations can prevent small problems from escalating into catastrophic failures. Components can be replaced or repaired before they cause larger system breakdowns. This approach reduces the frequency of major repairs and ensures that equipment operates at its optimal performance level for a longer period.

Implementing predictive maintenance is not without challenges. Data quality and reliability are crucial factors, as accurate predictions depend on high-quality sensor data. Data integration from different sources and legacy systems can be complex and may require investments in data infrastructure. Building and training accurate machine learning models demand data science and domain knowledge expertise. Moreover, predictive maintenance requires a cultural shift within organizations, transitioning from reactive firefighting to proactive planning.

The success of predictive maintenance hinges on the Internet of Things (IoT) and sensor technology. Sensors embedded in equipment gather data on factors like temperature, vibration, pressure, and performance metrics. IoT-enabled devices transmit this data in real-time, allowing predictive maintenance algorithms to detect anomalies and patterns. The proliferation of IoT devices and advancements in sensor technology have made predictive maintenance more accessible and cost-effective for various industries.

The trajectory of predictive maintenance is poised for further growth and innovation. As machine learning algorithms evolve, they become more adept at handling complex data and generating more accurate predictions. Predictive maintenance is not limited to manufacturing; it expands into industries like energy, transportation, and healthcare, where equipment uptime and reliability are essential. Predictive maintenance will continue to be integrated with broader digital transformation initiatives, leading to intelligent factories and interconnected systems that drive operational excellence.

Predictive maintenance in manufacturing epitomizes the synergy between data analytics, technology, and operational efficiency. By harnessing the power of data-driven insights, organizations can shift from reactive crisis management to proactive planning. Predictive maintenance optimizes operational costs, extends equipment lifespans, and empowers organizations to maximize their production potential. In an era of digital transformation, predictive maintenance is a testament to the transformative power of data-driven decision-making, paving the way for a future where factories and facilities operate with efficiency, precision, and proactive excellence.

Chapter XIII

Future Trends in
Data Science and Big Data

AI-driven Data Science

In the landscape of data-driven decision-making, the convergence of artificial intelligence (AI) and data science has brought about a transformative paradigm known as AI-driven data science. This fusion capitalizes on AI's ability to process, analyze, and learn from vast datasets, propelling data science to new heights of efficiency, accuracy, and innovation. AI-driven data science is not only reshaping how organizations extract value from their data but also revolutionizing industries, fueling breakthroughs in research, and enhancing human capabilities. This section explores the dynamic realm of AI-driven data science, delving into its key components, applications, challenges, and its profound impact on shaping the future of information-driven endeavors.

AI-driven data science represents a powerful synergy between two complementary disciplines. Data science encompasses the methodologies, tools, and techniques for extracting insights and knowledge from data. Conversely, AI empowers machines to perform tasks that traditionally require human intelligence, including pattern recognition, problem-solving, and decision-making. By integrating AI into data science workflows, organizations can automate and enhance processes, unlock hidden patterns, and gain predictive and prescriptive insights that drive strategic decision-making.

A cornerstone of AI-driven data science is machine learning—the subset of AI that empowers algorithms to learn from data and improve over time. Machine learning algorithms can automatically recognize complex patterns, correlations, and trends within vast datasets that would be challenging for humans to discern. Machine learning automates data cleaning, feature selection, and model-building tasks in data science. This automation accelerates analysis, reduces human error, and scales data science efforts to process immense datasets efficiently.

AI-driven data science elevates decision-making by offering predictive and prescriptive insights. Predictive analytics harnesses historical data and machine learning to forecast future trends, enabling organizations to anticipate customer behaviors, market shifts, and operational outcomes. Prescriptive analytics goes a step further, suggesting optimal actions based on predicted results. AI and data science fusion empowers organizations to make informed choices that drive strategic growth, resource allocation, and risk management.

AI-driven data science extends beyond numerical data to unstructured information like text. Natural Language Processing

(NLP) techniques enable machines to understand and interpret human language, unlocking valuable insights from textual sources like social media, customer reviews, and research articles. Text analytics combines NLP with data science methodologies to extract sentiment, identify themes, and extract actionable insights from textual data. AI-driven NLP automates text analysis and uncovers hidden patterns and sentiments that inform strategic decisions.

The impact of AI-driven data science transcends industry boundaries. In healthcare, AI analyzes medical images for early disease detection, assists in diagnosis, and aids in drug discovery. In finance, AI-driven algorithms predict market trends, detect fraudulent transactions, and optimize investment strategies. Manufacturing benefits from predictive maintenance, where AI analyzes sensor data to forecast equipment failures and optimize maintenance schedules. In retail, AI-driven data science drives personalized recommendations and demand forecasting, enhancing customer experiences.

While AI-driven data science holds transformative potential, it presents challenges rooted in the complexity of AI models and data integration. Ensuring the quality and integrity of training data is crucial, as biases within the data can lead to skewed results. Interpreting and explaining the outcomes of AI-driven models, often called the "black box" challenge, raises concerns about transparency and accountability. Moreover, the scarcity of AI expertise and the computational resources required for AI-driven data science can pose hurdles for organizations seeking to implement these approaches.

AI-driven data science raises ethical considerations concerning data privacy, bias, and accountability. As AI algorithms make decisions that impact individuals, the transparency of these decisions becomes paramount. Addressing bias in training data and algorithms is essential to prevent discriminatory outcomes. Organizations must prioritize ethical guidelines that respect individual rights and foster trust in AI-driven data science applications.

The future of AI-driven data science promises continual innovation and expansion. As AI technologies evolve, they will become more adept at handling complex data, accommodating varied sources and formats. Explainable AI—models that provide interpretable results—will enhance transparency and enable stakeholders to understand the reasoning behind AI-driven insights. As AI-driven data science matures, it will be instrumental in addressing global challenges, from healthcare breakthroughs to climate modeling, enabling informed decisions that shape a better future.

AI-driven data science emerges as a catalyst that empowers organizations to unlock hidden insights within their data and make informed, strategic decisions. The symbiotic relationship between AI and data science propels industries into an era of efficiency, innovation, and precision. By leveraging AI-driven insights, organizations gain predictive foresight, process automation, and actionable recommendations that amplify their competitive edge. As AI-driven data science continues to evolve, it is not just a tool— it is a transformative force that guides progress, accelerates innovation, and paves the way for a future where data-driven intelligence shapes every facet of our lives.

Edge Computing and IoT Data Analytics

In the landscape of technological advancement, the convergence of edge computing and Internet of Things (or IoT) data analytics has ignited a revolution that is redefining how data is processed, analyzed, and leveraged. As the proliferation of connected devices generates unprecedented volumes of data, the traditional model of centralizing data processing in remote data centers faces challenges of latency, bandwidth constraints, and security concerns. Edge computing emerges as a solution that shifts data processing closer to the source, enabling real-time insights, reduced latency, and improved efficiency. When combined with IoT data analytics, this paradigm creates a powerful synergy that empowers industries, enhances user experiences, and drives innovation. This section delves into the realm of edge computing and IoT data analytics, exploring their symbiotic relationship, applications, challenges, and the transformative impact they have on shaping the digital landscape.

Historically, data processing occurred in centralized data centers, where vast amounts of information were collected, stored, and analyzed. While this model served its purpose, the surge in data generated by IoT devices introduced challenges. Sending data to remote data centers for processing resulted in latency, network congestion, and delayed insights. Edge computing addresses these challenges by decentralizing data processing and moving it closer to the data source. This paradigm shift offers advantages like real-time processing, reduced data transmission, and improved scalability.

At the heart of edge computing lies the principle of proximity. Organizations can minimize data travel distances and associated delays by processing data at or near the source, whether it's a sensor, device, or gateway. This proximity translates into real-time insights, enabling rapid decision-making and event response. Edge computing is indispensable for applications requiring low latency, such as autonomous vehicles, industrial automation, and remote monitoring. Furthermore, edge computing optimizes bandwidth usage by transmitting only relevant data to central data centers, reducing network congestion.

IoT data analytics complements edge computing by transforming raw data into actionable insights. An extensive amount of data created by IoT devices holds immense potential, but its value is unlocked through meaningful analysis. IoT data analytics involves applying data science techniques to discover patterns, trends, and correlations within IoT-generated data. Machine learning algorithms identify anomalies, predict future events, and provide recommendations based on historical and real-time data. This intelligent analysis enriches decision-making, enhances operations, and enables proactive responses to emerging trends.

The marriage of edge computing and IoT data analytics has profound implications across diverse industries. Embedded sensors in manufacturing equipment produce real-time data that may be edge-analyzed to predict equipment breakdowns and optimize maintenance schedules. Smart cities leverage IoT data analytics to improve traffic management, enhance public safety, and optimize resource allocation. In healthcare, wearable devices capture patient data at the edge, enabling remote monitoring and personalized treatment plans. Agriculture benefits from edge computing by analyzing sensor data that monitors soil conditions, weather patterns, and crop health.

While the advantages of edge computing and IoT data analytics are substantial, they come with challenges that organizations must navigate. Ensuring data security at the edge is crucial, as decentralized processing introduces potential vulnerabilities. Data governance becomes complex, requiring organizations to define ownership, access controls, and compliance measures. The diverse range of IoT devices and data formats poses integration challenges that require standardized protocols and interoperability solutions. Organizations must also address scalability concerns, ensuring that edge computing infrastructure can handle the increasing volume of IoT-generated data.

Privacy considerations emerge as the edge becomes a focal point for data processing. Edge devices collect sensitive data, raising concerns about data ownership, consent, and the potential for unauthorized access. Organizations must implement robust encryption, authentication, and data anonymization measures to protect user privacy. Ethical considerations extend to data usage and transparency, ensuring that individuals are informed about how their data is being used and empowering them with control over their information.

The future of edge computing and IoT data analytics is marked by continued innovation and synergy with emerging technologies. Integrating 5G networks enhances edge computing capabilities by providing ultra-low latency and high bandwidth connectivity. The proliferation of edge AI, where AI models are deployed directly on edge devices, further accelerates real-time decision-making. The collaboration between edge computing, IoT, and AI will lead to smarter, more autonomous systems that enable dynamic, context-aware interactions.

Edge computing and IoT data analytics constitute a transformative paradigm that empowers organizations to harness the potential of data at the edge of innovation. By processing data near to the source, edge computing reduces latency, enhances efficiency, and unlocks real-time insights. IoT data analytics enriches this data by transforming it into actionable insights that drive informed decisions and enable proactive strategies. The synergy between edge computing and IoT data analytics permeates industries, from manufacturing and healthcare to smart cities and agriculture. As technology advances, the collaborative power of the intelligent edge will shape a future where connected devices, real-time insights, and autonomous systems redefine the boundaries of what is possible, propelling us into a world where data-driven intelligence is at our fingertips.

Ethical AI and Responsible Data Science

As the realms of artificial intelligence (AI) and data science continue to advance, the ethical implications of these technologies have come into sharper focus. Ethical AI and responsible data science encompass the principles, practices, and guidelines that guide the development, deployment, and use of AI and data-driven technologies in ways that prioritize human well-being, fairness, transparency, and accountability. The need for ethical considerations becomes paramount as AI systems make increasingly impactful decisions in domains like healthcare, finance, and criminal justice. This section explores the vital intersection of ethical AI and responsible data science, examining the challenges, principles, societal implications, and their crucial role in shaping a future where innovation and morality coexist harmoniously.

The rapid advancement of AI technologies has unveiled a spectrum of ethical difficulties that must be addressed. Bias in AI models, whether due to biased training data or algorithmic design, can perpetuate unfairness and discrimination. Transparency concerns arise as black-box AI models make decisions that are difficult to interpret or explain. Privacy issues surface when AI systems process personal data without consent or adequate safeguards. Moreover, the potential for AI to automate jobs and make high-stakes decisions, such as autonomous vehicles, raises ethical questions about accountability and human control.

Several core principles guide ethical AI and responsible data science practices. Fairness dictates that AI systems should be designed to avoid bias and provide equitable outcomes across diverse demographic groups. Transparency emphasizes the importance of making AI processes and decisions understandable and interpretable. Accountability holds developers and organizations responsible for the consequences of AI decisions. Privacy asserts the right of individuals to control their personal data and the necessity of informed consent. Finally, ensuring the benefit of humanity means that AI should be designed and used to enhance well-being and avoid harm.

Data ethics forms a cornerstone of responsible data science. Data collection, storage, and utilization must align with ethical principles to protect individuals' rights and maintain public trust. Data anonymization, where personal information is removed from datasets, mitigates privacy risks. Consent mechanisms ensure that individuals provide informed agreement before their data is used. Data stewardship involves transparently managing data to ensure its security, integrity, and proper usage. Ethical considerations extend to data sharing, where organizations balance openness with protecting sensitive information.

The societal implications of AI and data science are vast, spanning sectors from healthcare and education to criminal justice and finance. Bias in AI systems can lead to unfair outcomes, like discriminatory hiring practices or biased criminal sentencing. To mitigate bias, AI developers must ensure diverse and representative training data, employ bias-detection algorithms, and implement fairness-aware models that actively reduce disparities. Ethical considerations also dictate the need for continuous monitoring and updating of AI models to prevent the amplification of biases.

As the ethical landscape of AI evolves, the call for regulatory frameworks and policies has grown louder. Governments and organizations recognize the need to ensure that AI technologies are developed and deployed to protect individual rights and promote societal well-being. Regulations like the GDPR in Europe and discussions about AI ethics boards highlight the global effort to create guidelines that govern AI development, usage, and accountability.

Ethical AI and responsible data science education are pivotal in preparing professionals to navigate the complex terrain of AI ethics. Universities, organizations, and online platforms are introducing courses and resources that explore the ethical dimensions of AI, ensuring that developers, data scientists, and decision-makers understand the impact of their work on individuals and society. Ethical AI education fosters a culture of responsible innovation that seeks to balance technological advancement with moral considerations.

Ethical AI and responsible data science promise to create a technologically advanced world that values human dignity, fairness, and accountability. AI technologies prioritizing ethical principles can enhance healthcare diagnostics, promote inclusive education, and support environmental sustainability. Ethical AI can earn public trust and improve its societal impact by striving for transparency, fairness, and accountability.

Integrating ethical considerations becomes non-negotiable as AI and data science permeate every facet of modern life. Ethical AI and responsible data science serve as the moral compass that guides technological innovation, ensuring that human values and societal well-being remain at the forefront. By upholding fairness, transparency, accountability, and privacy principles, ethical AI transcends being a mere buzzword and evolves into a guiding philosophy that shapes a digital landscape where innovation aligns harmoniously with human ethics. In a world where technology's footprint is ubiquitous, ethical AI and responsible data science pave the way for a future where the power of innovation is harnessed for the greater good, enriching lives while safeguarding human dignity.

Conclusion

The Ever-Growing Importance of Data Science and Big Data Analytics

In the dynamic landscape of the 21st century, data has become the lifeblood of innovation, decision-making, and progress. The ever-growing importance of data science and big data analytics has ignited a transformative era where organizations, industries, and societies harness the power of data to uncover insights, drive efficiencies, and propel advancements. As data volume, velocity, and variety continue to surge, data science and big data analytics are essential tools in extracting meaningful patterns and knowledge from this wealth of information. This section explores the pivotal role that data science and big data analytics play today, examining their impact across diverse sectors, the challenges they address, and their integral role in shaping a future fueled by data-driven intelligence.

The digital age has ushered in an unprecedented data revolution, where the exponential growth of digital interactions generates constant information. Data is generated astonishingly from social media posts and e-commerce transactions to IoT sensors and scientific research. Data science, the interdisciplinary field that combines statistics, machine learning, and domain expertise, empowers us to extract insights from this data deluge. By applying mathematical models and algorithms to raw data, data science reveals hidden patterns, correlations, and trends that drive informed decision-making.

Big data analytics complements data science by providing the means to process and analyze vast datasets that exceed the capabilities of traditional tools. With the advent of technologies like Apache Hadoop and Spark, organizations can process terabytes, petabytes, and beyond cost-effectively and efficiently. Big data analytics uncovers insights that inform business strategies, scientific discoveries, and policy implementations. From customer behavior analysis in retail to genomic research in healthcare, big data analytics transforms raw data into actionable insights that propel industries forward.

The importance of data science and big data analytics transcends industry boundaries, manifesting their influence across sectors that range from healthcare and finance to transportation and entertainment. In healthcare, data-driven insights optimize patient care, enable personalized treatments, and facilitate early disease detection. Financial institutions utilize data analytics to detect fraudulent transactions, assess risk, and make investment decisions. Real-time sensor data enhances logistics, route optimization, and predictive maintenance in the transportation sector. The entertainment industry tailors content recommendations based on user preferences and viewing behaviors.

Data science and big data analytics address complex challenges that were once insurmountable. Climate modeling leverages vast datasets to predict weather patterns, understand environmental changes, and guide policy decisions. Criminal justice systems apply data analytics to predict crime hotspots, optimize resource allocation, and improve public safety. Agricultural practices benefit from precision farming, where data-driven insights guide irrigation, fertilization, and crop management, optimizing yields while conserving resources.

The importance of data science and big data analytics is accompanied by a set of challenges that require careful navigation. Privacy concerns arise as the collection and analysis of personal data become more pervasive. Ensuring data security and protecting sensitive information against breaches is a constant challenge. Bias in data and algorithms can lead to discriminatory outcomes, highlighting the importance of fair and transparent models. Additionally, the ethical use of data in domains like AI and surveillance demands responsible practices that respect individual rights and societal values.

As data evolves, unstructured data such as text, images, audio, and video presents a new frontier for exploration. Natural language processing (NLP) techniques enable the analysis of textual data from sources like social media, customer reviews, and scientific literature. Image and video analysis employ computer vision to derive insights from visual content. These advancements in unstructured data analysis enhance sentiment analysis, brand perception tracking, and content recommendation systems, enriching the depth and breadth of data-driven insights.

The ever-growing importance of data science and big data analytics heralds a future where data-driven decision-making becomes ubiquitous. Organizations that harness data-driven insights gain a competitive advantage by understanding customer preferences, optimizing processes, and predicting trends. Integrating AI and machine learning amplifies the power of data science, enabling autonomous systems and intelligent decision support. With the proliferation of IoT devices, data generation will continue to surge, necessitating sophisticated analytics to transform this data into valuable insights.

In the information age, data science and big data analytics are catalysts that drive innovation, empower industries, and shape societies. They transform raw data into actionable insights that enhance decision-making, drive efficiencies, and propel advancements across diverse sectors. The ever-growing importance of data science and big data analytics creates a landscape where organizations that harness data-driven intelligence gain a competitive edge and contribute to a future enriched by informed progress. As we navigate this data-centric era, ethical considerations, responsible practices, and continuous learning will be pivotal in maximizing the potential of data science and big data analytics to fuel a more intelligent, interconnected, and innovative world.

Encouragement for Further Learning and Exploration

In the ever-evolving landscape of knowledge and innovation, pursuing further learning and exploration remains a transformative endeavor that enriches our lives and expands our horizons. The continuous learning journey transcends traditional boundaries, offering opportunities to acquire new skills, deepen existing knowledge, and explore uncharted territories. It is a testament to human curiosity, adaptability, and the innate desire to grow intellectually, professionally, and personally. This section seeks to ignite the flame of encouragement for further learning and exploration, emphasizing the myriad benefits, avenues, and strategies that pave the way for a lifelong journey of discovery and growth.

Learning is a never-ending process that happens throughout life. The need to continuously learn and adapt is greater than ever in this age of fast technological innovation. The science, technology, arts, and humanities fields offer a wide range of topics for investigation and comprehension since they are ever-evolving. The information we learn now might prove to be a starting point for future discoveries and insights that are much more profound. We are encouraged to leave our comfort zones and take on new challenges with an open mind and an inquisitive spirit by this dynamic learning environment.

The transformative power of curiosity lies at the heart of further learning and exploration. Curiosity is the engine that propels us to ask questions, seek answers, and dive into the depths of knowledge. It is a force that defies complacency and drives us to challenge assumptions, unravel complexities, and discover innovative solutions. By nurturing our innate curiosity, we embark on a journey of intellectual growth that enhances our understanding of the world and fuels our passion for lifelong learning.

The benefits of further learning extend far beyond the acquisition of knowledge. Lifelong learning cultivates critical thinking skills, enabling us to analyze information, evaluate sources, and make informed decisions. It fosters adaptability, allowing us to thrive in dynamic environments and navigate change with resilience. Moreover, learning broadens our perspectives, exposing us to diverse cultures, ideas, and experiences that enrich our empathy and understanding of others. As we embrace continuous learning, we develop a sense of fulfillment, empowerment, and a deeper connection to the world.

The avenues for further learning and exploration are vast and varied. Traditional educational institutions offer formal courses, degrees, and certifications that provide structured learning experiences. However, the digital age has democratized learning, offering a wealth of online resources, tutorials, and platforms that cater to diverse interests and schedules. Podcasts, webinars, virtual workshops, and e-learning platforms enable us to delve into subjects ranging from data science and art history to philosophy and sustainable living. Additionally, reading books, attending conferences, joining clubs, and engaging in peer discussions are avenues that foster intellectual growth and discovery.

There are many happy and fulfilling moments along the way as one pursues more education and discovery. The feeling of mastering a new skill, grasping a complex concept, or solving a challenging problem is gratifying. Each step forward represents personal growth and an investment in our potential to contribute positively to our communities and the world at large. The journey itself becomes a source of inspiration as we continuously expand our boundaries and unlock new layers of understanding.

The journey of lifelong learning is challenging. Time constraints, competing priorities, and self-doubt can be hurdles to overcome. Yet, every challenge presents an opportunity for growth. By setting clear goals, creating a structured learning plan, and fostering a growth mindset, we can navigate these challenges with determination. Cultivating a supportive network of peers, mentors, and like-minded individuals also provides encouragement and accountability on this journey.

In conclusion, encouraging further learning and exploration invites us to embrace the spirit of discovery that resides within us all. Pursuing knowledge, skills, and experiences is a journey transcending age, background, and circumstances. It is a journey that nurtures our intellectual curiosity, empowers us with adaptability, and enriches our lives with a deeper understanding of the world. Whether we engage in formal education, online courses, self-directed learning, or a combination of these avenues, the act of continuously seeking new horizons is a testament to our commitment to growth, enrichment, and the unwavering pursuit of excellence. As we set out on this adventure, let us keep in mind that acquiring knowledge is an investment in oneself as well as a celebration of the infinite possibilities of the human mind and the astounding wonders of the world we live in.

Thank you for buying and reading/listening to our book. If you found this book useful/helpful please take a few minutes and leave a review on the platform where you purchased our book. Your feedback matters greatly to us.